[THE SECRET TO SELLING MORE]

INSTITUTE FOR MARKETING AND INNOVATION   SANTA CLARA, CA

[THE SECRET TO SELLING MORE]

It's Not Where You've Been Looking,
If It Were, You'd Have Found It Already

by Mitchell Goozé

ISBN 1-889772-06-2
Library of Congress Catalog Number 00-134195

Designed by London Road Design
Printed in the United States of America

2 3 4 5 6 7 8 9 10

[TO M. TED STEINBERG]

[ACKNOWLEDGEMENTS]

The Secret to Selling More is my second book on the topic of marketing and sales. This volume evolved out of the frustrations my clients and I have experienced while working together over the past several years. Many of my insights came from helping them increase sales.

I want to thank Kathleen Gill and Bayard Bookman for their willingness to read early drafts of the manuscript and for providing valuable direction. Thanks also to Donna Young, Lawren Farber, and Liz Miller for their input and help in crafting a better product, to Jeff Krawitz for suggestions on tone and content and to David Palmer for his editorial suggestions that proved very helpful. I also want to thank my wife, Carol, who helped with the final editing of the galleys.

Last, and certainly not least, I want to acknowledge the life-long work and thinking of Ted Steinberg, SPE*. Ted

* Self-Proclaimed Expert

and I have been collaborating for 16 years on our marketing and sales thinking. While we don't always agree on the details, we certainly agree on the philosophy. Ted has provided guidance and concepts, through his construct of The Ultimate Selling Machine, which I might never have discovered, without his annoying perseverance.

[CONTENTS]

[INTRODUCTION]

Are you happy with the performance of your sales force[1]? OK, that's an unfair question — because you can almost always use more sales. However, are all, or even most, of your sales people performing as well as your top performer(s)? Are they coming even close?

In this book I'm going to examine two methods for improving the performance of your sales organization. The first method looks at efficiency, and the second looks at effectiveness. (Just to be clear: *Efficiency* is doing things right; *Effectiveness* is doing the right things.)

---

1. A note on capitalization: Due to the confusing use of terms, I will capitalize the words "sales" and "marketing" when the words are used without a modifier and I am referring to the Sales and Marketing Departments within a company. Otherwise the terms will not be capitalized. For example: sales force and marketing department are not capitalized since the words "force" and "department" are there to clarify. "How are sales?" or "What marketing do you provide?" don't have "sales" and "marketing" capitalized because I'm not referring to the respective departments. "What's going on in Sales or Marketing" does have those two words capitalized since I'm referring to the respective departments or organizations and have not included the clarifying word.

And what do I mean by "performance" of your sales organization? Performance of an individual sales professional can be measured in a number of ways. These include, and are certainly not limited to:

Gross or net sales dollars

Gross or net margin dollars

Share of customer

Percentage of possible accounts served

The performance of the entire sales organization is then the sum of the performances of the individual sales people within the organization. Therefore, to improve the performance of Sales, you need to improve the performance of some — or better yet most — of your sales people.

Improved efficiency can be measured by either the increase in Sales' performance at the same or lower cost of selling, or by achieving the same Sales' performance at a lower cost of selling. Improved effectiveness indicates Sales' ability to sell more of the "right" customers "right." Knowing who the right customers are clearly impacts

Sales' ability to increase effectiveness. And in the same vein, knowing what "selling them right" means is equally important to effectiveness. Increasing efficiency and/or effectiveness can improve the performance of your sales people and your company.

However, as in most sales organizations, the probability is that the performance of your individual sales people follows a bell curve. That so-called normal performance distribution is shown in Figure 1. Does the performance curve of your sales organization have to be that way?

Before answering this question, consider a related, and possibly a more disturbing one. Has the absolute sales performance of your entire sales organization, measured in

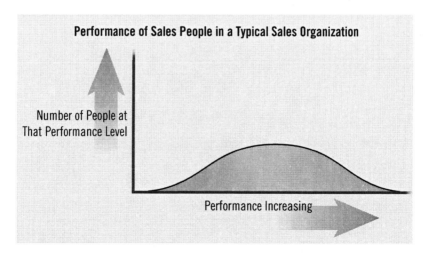

Performance of Sales People in a Typical Sales Organization

Number of People at That Performance Level

Performance Increasing

Figure 1.

sales dollars or margin dollars per sales person (or other similar measure), improved in real dollars (adjusted for inflation) over the last five, ten, or twenty years? If it has, is the improvement significant? Had your manufacturing or service delivery efficiency improved only as much as your selling productivity[2], would you still be in business?

If the previous questions got your attention, read on, because you'll find some eye-opening solutions to these problems as you go forward. No matter what your company sells — consumer products, high-tech, low-tech, or no-tech industrial products — or if you're in the services business, the solutions will be revealed.

If you don't see a real sales performance disparity between most of your sales people and your few top performers, and if your sales organization's overall productivity is moving upward significantly, then you can stop reading now because you don't need this book.

The Value of Training

Most companies, and the people in those companies,

---

2. Productivity is a measurement of Sales' ability to sell efficiently and effectively. Doing the wrong things well doesn't increase productivity.

attempt to improve the selling skills of their sales people the same way that companies usually attack a perceived skill deficiency, through training. Management's belief is generally that if performance is below expectations, and it appears that better skills are required, then training is often the identified solution. However, "training," as the preferred solution to people problems, goes in and out of favor with management.

Training and continuous improvement of the people in the company have been de rigueur for enlightened management — this time around — for more than a decade. In fact, sales training is the largest category for training investment made by companies. But to what end?

If the objective of all this training is to improve selling skills — and ultimately increase the sales of your company's products or services — why hasn't it worked? OK, it's had some effect. But in reality there's still a wide disparity between your best producers and the "rest of the pack." And your overall selling productivity hasn't increased in real terms. So this training that you're hanging your hat on, what effect has it had?

Don't feel too badly, my research suggests you're in a very large boat with lots of company.

Almost by unanimous consent, the vast majority of the more than 2,000 company executives I've talked with over the last nine years express dissatisfaction with the performance of their sales force. Beyond the limited number of top performers in each organization, there is a substantial drop-off in the performances of the rest of the sales force. And this pattern transcends company size or industry type.

Even if you want to stubbornly cling to the premise that a bell shaped performance curve is inevitable with any organization, the standard deviation from the mean[3] performance of your sales people doesn't have to continue to be as wide as it is. Compare the difference between the 'flat' bell curve in Figure 1 and the curve in Figure 2.

For those less mathematically inclined, this means the curve doesn't have to continue to be as flat as it is in Figure 1: the difference in performance between the top

---

3.   Just to be clear, the mean is the point at which half of the sales people have a better performance and half have performance that is worse. It is not necessarily the average, but rather the mid-point performance level at which half the people are better and half are worse.

performers and the mean should be less. Both Figure 1 and Figure 2 show a normal or bell-shaped distribution. The important contrast is the degree of performance difference between the top producers and the mean[4] in Figure 1 (a large difference) and in Figure 2 (a substantially smaller difference).

Also, there's no excuse for the overall performance of the sales organization not improving significantly over time when given an investment in useful education and training. That is, even if the distribution curve remained flatter than you'd like, the total performance of

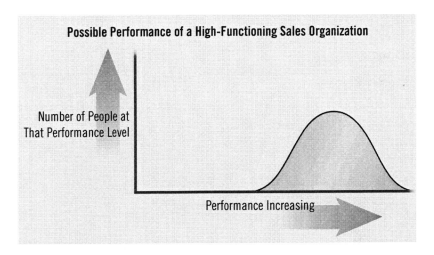

Possible Performance of a High-Functioning Sales Organization

Number of People at That Performance Level

Performance Increasing

Figure 2.

4.　Even though the mean is the half-way point in performance, there is nothing that says the difference between the top producer and the mean or middle producer needs to be large.

the organization should improve. In other words, the mean and average sales level per sales person should increase more than the rate of inflation. The total curve should move to the right, which indicates a higher level of sales per sales person.

If you review Figure 3 (where the performance curves from Figures 1 and 2 have been combined into one graph for easier comparison), you can see that the overall performance indicated by the second curve is not only higher, but the variance between the higher performance people and the median is less when compared to the original curve.

But, this type of sales performance improvement, as indicted by the second curve, has not occurred despite a

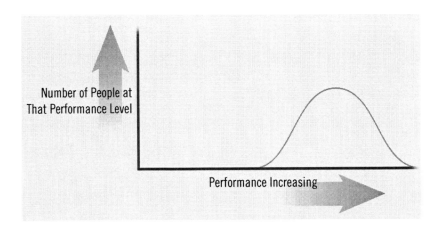

Figure 3.

monumental investment in sales training by companies across a multitude of industries over many, many years.

How Big Is This Problem?

Improving the performance of sales people is not a trivial problem. Large sums of money and resources are spent every year attempting to increase sales performance. To help you understand the difficulty that's been encountered trying to solve this problem, let's look at some numbers. Since the year 1900, over 6,000 books about selling have been published in North America. Just since 1990 there have been over 1,000 new ones. Any competently written book — and even some incompetently written books — about selling sells.

At any given time, a reasonably stocked bookstore can have more than 50 titles dealing with improving selling. Millions of copies of these books have been sold. Presumably the purchaser's intention has been to improve their selling skills or the skills of their sales people.

Corporations and individuals spend billions of dollars every year on sales training with an eye towards improving efficiency and effectiveness. With what results? If the gap between the great sales people and the rest of the pack isn't closing; if a larger number of sales people aren't falling into the "great" category; and if the overall sales organization is not really improving, then what's the point? With apologies to Zig Ziglar, Tom Hopkins, Wilson Learning and the countless others who offer popular sales training programs, but it's still very under-populated "at the top" — Why?

Certainly selling well is a skill — one that needs to be mastered. With all the attention paid to training and improving the skill level of the hundreds of thousands of practitioners of this profession, and the opportunity to practice daily, you'd think companies' sales performances would be improving. You would also expect those companies to be happy with their sales organizations. Yet this isn't the case. So, given the disappointing results of such investments, why do top managers continue to throw resources in this direction?

What's the Upside?

The potential upside from increased sales by the majority of your sales force is also not trivial. This potential is undoubtedly the single biggest factor behind throwing money at the problem. In fact, it's easy to estimate this upside.

A few years ago, *Selling Power* magazine described an eye-opening mathematical exercise that can quickly demonstrate the potential for moving the vast middleground of your sales people from acceptable to great. The process of quantification works as follows:

1. Identify your top sales producer

2. Quantify his or her sales per year

3. Multiply that figure by the number of full-time equivalent sales people you employ

4. The resulting figure is a close approximation of the sales you could have — if you could just teach the rest of your sales people to sell like your best performer

For most companies this calculated upside is more than double their current sales. (I have seen upsides approaching 10x.) No wonder you keep trying to improve Sales' performance! You can also use this calculation to help you know which performance curve (Figure #1 or Figure #2) more closely approximates your current sales organization's performance.

If your calculated upside is 2x or more than your current sales, your sales organization's performance approximates Figure #1. If, on the other hand, your calculated upside is less than 2x your current sales, then your sales organization's performance has a tighter curve such as the one shown in Figure #2.

There is, unfortunately, one very important caveat to that statement. While you may, in fact, have a tighter sales performance curve, it could be that your median performance is actually low rather than high. In other words, you may have a closely performing group of low-performance individuals rather than a closely performing group of high-performance people. (See Figure 4)

So What's the Solution?

Since countless books have been written to show you ways of increasing sales, I am not going to rehash what they've said. Instead I show you why all of that 'stuff' hasn't worked. Before we can get to that point however, a review of other important issues involved with increasing sales is in order.

This book is divided into two sections. "Section 1: Increasing Sales Efficiency" reviews efficiency-based solu-

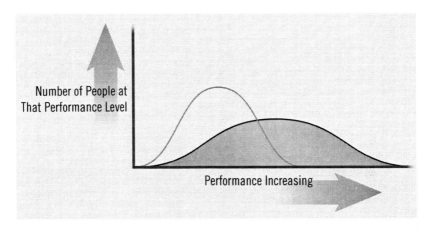

Figure 4.

tions for increasing sales. That is, how to get more sales from the same, or less, selling expense. Under this section, "The Efficiency Solution (Part 1)" looks at an organizational model that has been proven in countless industries to increase sales and lower selling expenses. If you're already using this solution in your business and don't need to know more about it, you can skip to "The Efficiency Solution (Part 2)" which begins on page 47.

"The Efficiency Solution (Part 2)" reviews how the Internet and related technologies can increase selling efficiency in your company. Following that, comes yet another efficiency solution — sales force automation, also known as customer relationship management. This is covered in "The Efficiency Solution (Part 3)" which begins on page 55.

These efficiency solutions are covered briefly, because, while they are very valuable and useful, they aren't the *real* secret to increasing sales. That's covered in "Section 2: The Secret — Revealed" which begins on page 69. You may be tempted to skip "The Efficiency Solution" to get to the real secret. You can if you want to, but you'll miss a number of valuable ideas. The ideas presented in Section 1 work in and of themselves. They also complement the secret revealed in Section 2.

[SECTION ONE]

INCREASING SALES
EFFICIENCY

Business is always a struggle . . . Every winner has scars . . .
The men who succeed are the efficient few.

Herbert Casson

There can be no economy where there is no efficiency.

Benjamin Disraeli

It is more than probable that the average man could, with no
injury to his health, increase his efficiency fifty percent.

Walter Scott

Efficiency is doing things — not wishing you could do them,
dreaming about them, or wondering if you can do them.

Frank Crane

The test of efficiency is the length of time it takes you to find out
when you're wrong.

Anonymous

Obviously, the highest type of efficiency is that which can utilize
existing material to the best advantage.

Jawaharlal Nehru

Luck is infatuated with the efficient.

Persian Proverb

[PART ONE]

THE EFFICIENCY SOLUTION

[THE EFFICIENCY SOLUTION]

(Part 1)

Before We Get Started

Just a reminder, efficiency is doing things right. Effectiveness is doing the right thing.

How About Another Process?

You are faced with the conundrum of having spent large sums of money on conventional and modern methods to increase sales, which brought no real results, and the urgent, continuing need to increase sales productivity. Some smart companies have taken another approach to solve the problem of their insufficient sales performance.

In addition to implementing sales training programs, these companies have also attempted to redefine their selling process to make it more efficient — and therefore less costly.

If you can't materially improve the performance of individual sales people or the sales organization as a whole, can you find a sales process that reduces the cost of selling? This question is one of the drivers that has pushed innovative companies to open their minds.

Regardless of whether you buy into the ultimate premise to make more of your sales people great — and it will be discussed in more detail in Section 2 because it needs a lot more discussion — it's important to find an efficient selling process that maximizes effectiveness while minimizing costs. Sales efficiency is a less controversial subject than the "best way to sell." So, what are smart companies doing to achieve higher Sales efficiency?

Willy Loman Revisited

Given the original paradigm for professional sales, you had to be in front of the buyer, pressing the flesh, to make the sale. People buy from people they like, so get out there and get liked! Modern, "solution selling," "consultative selling," or "Spin selling" models modify the old paradigm. They suggest that sales professionals should add value to the sales process.

This approach is good — but who says you have to be face-to-face to add value?

In the "old days" selling territories were limited by the sales person's ability to travel by foot, horse, or whatever. Pasquale Pistorio, the president of ST Microelectronics, told a story when he was vice-president of sales at Motorola Semiconductor. He recounted how he covered his sales territory in Italy by bicycle. The advent of the train, automobile, and airplane has expanded the potential territory of the professional sales person. However, as efficiency boosters, these transportation-based territory expanders are trivial when compared to the real paradigm shift that's possible.

The Face-to-Face Myth

Who says that to be effective all or even most of the steps in the sales process need to be accomplished face-to-face? This idea may be a radical or even heretical concept for some of you. After all, *real* sales professionals carry a brief-case and drive a car. Conducting the sales process to any material extent exclusively by mail, e-mail, or phone — well, that's for non-professional sales people. You know — telemarketers.

Think again. What's in it for the customer when your sales people show up most of the time? — Lunch? In real-ity your sales person's presence at the customer's site usu-ally adds no real value from the customer's perspective. You don't agree? Ask your customers, if you have the guts. And be sure to keep an open mind, and don't even think about saying "yeah, but" to any of their comments.

If you want an even quicker calibration, ask yourself how many of your suppliers' sales people add value by coming to your company as often as they do. Why do you think your customers or prospects view your sales people any differently?

If you're willing to learn from others, consider this. The March 1998 issue of *Marketing Tools* contained an arti-cle entitled "Face Time." The article stated that a recent con-fidential study by a $2.2B company found that 50% of their customers could not recall whether the sales contact was face-to-face or by phone only five days after the contact.

Want more proof? According to the same article, Arthur Anderson has been surveying the marketplace since 1970 by asking for opinions on the relative importance of various "values" provided by companies. The valuable items, in the order of their perceived value, included among others:

1. Contact with outside salesperson

2. Frequency and speed of delivery

3. Price

4. Range of products available

5. Capable inside sales person

This above list is in the order of the item's importance in 1970. The survey was conducted in 1980, 1985 and 1990. In each survey the value of inside sales has gone up, and the value of outside sales visits has gone down. The prioritized list in 1990 looked like this:

1. Capable inside salesperson

2. Frequency and speed of delivery

3. Range of products available

4. Price

▼

8. Contact with outside sales person

Note that "contact with outside sales person" had dropped from #1 to #8, while capable inside sales person had climbed from #5 to #1. Isn't it time for you to reconsider the face-to-face myth in your business?

Maybe you take the position that your sales people need to be there for *your* company's benefit. You learn things about the customer you could never learn without having someone physically present. Yes, that's probably true, and face-to-face contact can be very valuable. In turn, it's sometimes valuable to the customer for your sales people to visit in person. The problem is that your sales people are probably meeting customers and prospects face-to-face too often. And due to their face-to-face selling paradigm bias, they are using the phone, fax, e-mail, and snail-mail much too little.

The good news is, if you change the process you don't have to change their bias! If they've been trained right —

I'll get to what I mean by right in Section 2 — and they're good at what they do, the best way for them to add value in the solution-based, consultative, value-added, or similar sales model, is to sell face-to-face. It's just that they can effectively handle many more accounts (which increases efficiency) if you first change how your company manages its sales process.

A More Efficient Model

Forward thinking companies have discovered that by modifying the sales process to include telephone-based sales professionals, they can achieve a dramatic, positive increase in sales per sales professional. And this increase comes at a lower cost per sales professional.

The savings these companies experience is not due to telephone-based people making less money; if these sales people are as good as they should be, they won't make much less. The savings come from a more efficient sales force and from lower operating expenses per sales person. Inside sales people don't have travel costs, cars, cellular phones, field offices, or expense accounts.

Increased sales force efficiency results from the synergy (look, if I'm going to throw in "paradigm," you had to know "synergy" couldn't be far behind) created by an inside sales professional and an outside sales professional working together in a process designed to optimize the skills of each.

The typical field-based sales professional makes, at most, three to six sales calls a day and makes very inefficient use of the telephone. Remember, within their paradigm, face-to-face is what it takes. A good inside sales professional can make ten to twenty-five true sales "visits" per day without ever leaving their desk. These telephone visits can eliminate many of the non-value-added face-to-face visits that have been wasting your field sales people's time, and that have also increased your cost of selling. This modified process really works.

Before I get into some real world examples, take a look at Figure 5. This maps a simplified sales process. There may be numerous intermediate steps within each of these major steps depending upon the variables in the buying process of your particular industry's customers. How can you communicate more efficiently with potential customers at the various points in this process? There are going to be trade-offs in effectiveness as you try to become more efficient. Those trade-offs have to be measured and managed to improve performance and/or lower costs. How do you do that?

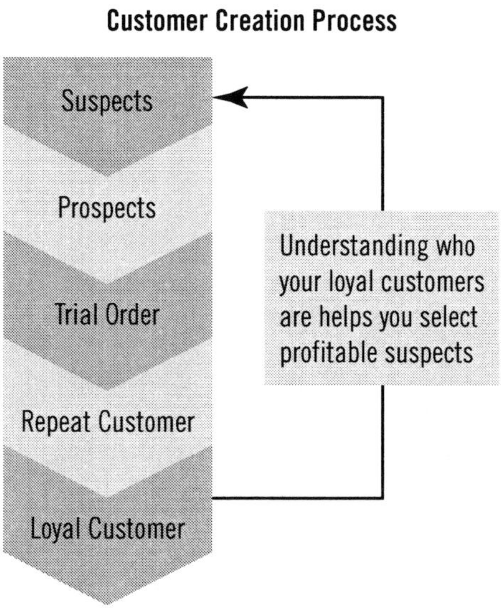

Customer Creation Process

Figure 5.

Try thinking of the sales process as a manufacturing process. What are you trying to manufacture? — loyal, profitable customers. How well are you doing it? How can you improve a production process you haven't yet defined? Do you see the problem? You can't expect to get better on purpose without a process you can manage.

To become more efficient at selling, you must be willing to truly understand the customer's own buying process and then design a selling process that matches his or her needs. It is foolish trying to sell to the customer the way you want to sell. Understand how they buy first, and then adapt your selling process to match their buying process.

Everything you own that you're sorry you purchased, somebody sold you. The stuff you love — you yourself bought. So, to sell correctly, you must help the right customers buy.

The selling process can be designed only once the customer's buying process is understood. Once you open your mind to new design possibilities, you can change the resources you apply to managing the process. These changes increase efficiency, lower costs — and usually are more effective too.

Selling Business-to-Business, High Ticket

Now, let me give you some real world examples. I'll start with a business-to-business sale of a high-ticket item. In the early 1980s, I ran a computer workstation company that sold $25,000 to $50,000 systems. (While workstation prices have dropped dramatically since then, in today's environment and for the usage envisioned, this is about a $100,000 sale in today's dollars.) Conventional wisdom held that to be able to sell to the *Fortune* 100 IT departments, which we were targeting, required a field sales organization of national scope. This organization was expected to hand-hold customers and provide additional field support on-site as needed.

Field support people were necessary back then. However, with today's technology and smart, self-diagnostic products, the need for as many field-based support people is being minimized. They can now connect the engine control computer in your car, via cellular phone and the Internet, to a remote diagnostic service center. This new use of technology will help you determine whether the 'check engine' light indicates an imminent catastrophe or if it can be ignored until you get to a repair center.

Back to our 1980s example. The field sales organization, which was very limited due to the company's start-up nature, was neither fully effective nor truly national in scope. (There were employees in some cities in the United States, but in contrast to truly national companies, it was far from effective coverage.) But the organization still cost a lot of money. Unfortunately, I failed to discover, until we'd run through too much money, that we could have executed a substantial portion of the sales process over the telephone.

Not knowing the end was near, the company converted to a combination of inside and outside sales people. Using telephone-based sales professionals in combination with the field sales people, we were able to place five times as many trial orders for the product in only 20% of the time.

If we could have discovered sooner how to sell more efficiently, the company might have survived its investor crisis. As sales consultant Jay Shelov likes to say, "A 40% increase in sales will hide a multitude of sins."

Selling Through Distributors or Retailers

How about a business-to-channel strategy? In the mid-1980s, Ted Steinberg ran a company called 10-Star that sold personal computer diskettes and other accessories through retailers. His competitors sold exclusively through field sales people who were either company employees or manufacturer's representatives.

Ted's business used telesales people only. His sales people signed on new dealers and serviced them over the telephone. Rarely did a sales person visit a dealer. 10-Star became very successful at establishing new dealers, and at understanding their stocking needs without much, if any, face time. This isn't necessarily the perfect business model. It's just what the thinly capitalized company could afford — and it worked. Today a combination of inside sales people and outside merchandisers or detailers, with some sales background, could be the right mix for this type of business.

Changing the Rules, Winning the Market

Then, there's the printed circuit board manufacturing company in the Pacific Northwest. This company has become one of the largest U.S. suppliers of printed circuit boards to OEMs (original equipment manufacturers) by exclusively using inside sales people. And that arrangement came about by accident.

Well, not exactly. When they started, the company couldn't afford field sales people. They decided to temporarily use inside sales people until they could afford 'real' sales people. None of their competitors utilized inside sales people, except for taking orders or providing customer service. They ultimately expected to follow the sales and support model of their competitors, but they made this professional compromise and used only tele-sales people to get the business going.

The company soon discovered what numerous smart companies have also realized. When done right, inside sales works — and it costs a lot less than a field sales organization. A few years ago when I met with this company they had become a leader in the industry and had yet to hire a full-time, outside sales professional. They discovered that properly trained inside sales people could serve their customers better and at a lower cost. Additionally, they made more sales per person. They went from start-up to leader in less than five years.

But We're a Retailer

The same arrangement works in retail. Look at how many successful retailers have added catalog operations to their sales process in recent years. What's a catalog except an efficient way to reach customers who can't, won't, or just don't shop in your store? Not only that, but it's been proven that a catalog will often stimulate a customer to come into the store. Look at this: inside sales (in this case mail-based rather than telephone-based) becomes the first step towards making a successful face-to-face sale.

OK, What Makes It Work?

Why does inside sales, or a combination of inside sales and outside sales professionals, work so well? From the customer's viewpoint, consider the major job of the sales person. Customers expect the sales person to represent their concerns to the company and to solve their problems, though not necessarily in that order.

Viewing the sales person's responsibility from this perspective, where are the solutions to most of your customers' problems? That's right, at your factory, head-quarters, or service support center. Many times when a sales person is asked a question or needs to provide help to the customer, they must turn to headquarters for the answer.

So what does the sales person do? They call and hope to find the right person who can and will provide the customer with the help required. Providing the solution is so much easier if you're already located at headquarters. Think about all the problems your sales people are able to 'run down' on their periodic visits to headquarters.

In some cases the solution to the customer's problem requires on-their-site expertise from your company. Is that really the appropriate role for your sales people? Would a field technical specialist be better to have on site? I'll grant you that sometimes it could be the right role for your field sales person. It's just that by teaming that field person with an inside sales professional, they are likely to be a lot more efficient. This teamwork approach allows the field sales person to spend their time in such a way that their on-site presence really adds value for both you and your customer.

Most of the time the value added by the sales professional comes from their providing the customer with

THE SECRET TO SELLING MORE

solutions to a particular problem. When problems are more technical or specific, the sales person needs to have the appropriate skills. But, the personality requirements that come with technical problem-solving skills are often incompatible with the personality type that's the consummate sales person. A sales team can resolve this dichotomy.

This synergistic relationship is well understood by larger companies. They often team field sales professionals with a field technical or product specialist. Do your top sales people really need to be in the field full-time? Your honest answer to this question could lead you to a better selling system for your company.

It Even Works in High Tech

Let me give you an example of teamwork in the real world. When I was president of Teledyne Semiconductor, we followed a traditional field sales model in our selling process. The company had been in business for over 25 years (it was the third commercial semiconductor company to be started after Fairchild and Signetics). For as many years as we had kept accurate records, sales for the company had pretty much followed the industry growth curve for each region of the world. That is, our sales in North America went up or down in any given year with the rest of the industry's sales in North America. Similarly we also stayed in line with industry sales in Europe and Asia.

I joined Teledyne Semiconductor in 1985. For my first two years with the company we continued to enjoy the same follow-the-tide, go-with-the-flow, results. In 1987 we changed our sales model and began using a combination of field sales engineers and inside sales professionals. To my knowledge, no other semiconductor company at that time had tried to use inside, outbound, sales professionals as the primary sales connection with the customer.

Numerous people told me this model wouldn't work. However, given the capital constraints presented by Teledyne, and my predecessors' failures to capitalize on the company's previous pioneering innovations, I wasn't left with very many attractive options. And 'more of the same' wasn't going to get us where we needed to go.

One year after implementing this team-based sales process just in North America, we had the first occurrence of sales in a region that didn't match the industry's growth curve for that same North American region — they far *exceeded* it. Our North American sales growth for that year was double the growth of the rest of the semi-conductor industry as a whole. The company also showed more growth in North America than for any other region. And at a lower selling cost. Some skeptics still thought our success was an anomaly. The next year we implemented a similar system in Europe which yielded equally good results.

But It Won't Work in *My* Business

Of course, you can choose to ignore the above examples. And you may decide that inside sales (including telesales, teleprospecting, telequalifying, direct mail, catalog sales, etc.) "won't work in your business." Well, you'd better hope you're right — or that all your current and future competitors agree with you. All I can say in response to that mind-set is *good luck*. I say that because there's a very high probability, based on real-world market evidence, that you're dead wrong.

[PART TWO]

THE EFFICIENCY SOLUTION

[THE EFFICIENCY SOLUTION]

(Part 2)

The Internet to the Rescue

The Internet is another tool that forward-thinking companies have added to their sales process in an attempt to increase sales or lower selling costs. Enhanced communication between people at a distance — from the Pony Express to the telegraph to the telephone to fax and now to the Internet — have all been breakthroughs for increasing sales efficiency. Understanding fully how to apply each new tool to the sales process has created major opportunities for innovative companies over the years. Without question, the Internet represents the greatest tool for changing the sales process since the invention of the telephone 100 years ago.

To appreciate exactly what the Internet can do for your company and its sales, and exactly how it can work for you, requires your time and attention. You have to use it, try it, and experiment with it to learn. The cost is minimal to get involved with the Net. And its use is the only way you'll learn how it can work for you. If you're not using it today, I wouldn't wait until tomorrow.

A few quick examples follow on how the Net today (2005) can support sales. (I don't want to go too far with this because by the time you read this book, given the speed with which the Internet is evolving, these examples could be old hat.)

ET Phone Home

Enzymatic Therapy is a natural medicine company based in Green Bay, Wisconsin. The Internet provides consumers, medical professionals, and retailers with up-to-date scientific information about natural alternatives to traditional medical treatments. People with access to the Net can download valuable information about complementary and alternative medicines and can also ask questions of medical and scientific professionals on the Enzymatic Therapy website (www.enzy.com).

Prior to the Internet, the company could only afford to provide this information to their sales force. The sales people had to copy these medical abstracts and related information, and then bring or mail the copies to the retailer or medical professional. The retailer or medical professional then had to pass this information on to the customer/patient who originally prompted the question. This drawn out process took a lot of time and effort on the part of many people. But the company knew that the information was critical to the sales process, and helped the right customers buy right.

The Internet allows Enzymatic Therapy to provide this valuable information world-wide, 24-hours a day, seven days a week and much more cost effectively than before. And the website is available to a vastly larger audience of retailers, medical professionals and consumers. And this is all happening from Green Bay, Wisconsin!

And, of Course, a High-Tech Example

National Semiconductor, a Santa Clara-based semiconductor ("chip") supplier, discovered a novel way to utilize the Internet to keep their product managers informed of market interest in their products.

Their website gets thousands of "hits" per day from engineers and other technical people who need information about National's products. National tracks these hits and other product-focused demands, and then provides that information to the various product managers using National's Intranet and push technology. This inquiry data, combined with distributor point-of-sale information from around the world, is added to traditional daily or weekly shipment data. Each product manager, anywhere in the world, can access this information in real-time. The data is then formatted to provide valuable information that the product manager can use to forecast demand, and match future production to the trends.

Selling Over the Net

Dell Computer pioneered the sale of personal computers over the phone. (Now in Part 1 of this Section, I could have used Dell to illustrate how a more efficient sales method changed the sales model for the computer industry forever.) When Michael Dell started his company in 1984, enlightened thinkers said that to sell computers one needed a face-to-face presence, either at the retail level, or at your company site, to "close the deal." Dell's success changed that thinking forever. And now they've expanded to the Internet. When the first edition of this book was written in 2000, Dell Computer was selling over $20,000,000 in computers per *day* over the Internet. Today they sell vastly more than that.

The Internet allows Dell, and other companies, to accept orders via computer without a sales professional interacting with the customer during the buying process. This obviously reduces the cost of selling. Their foray into Internet selling could have reduced sales if not done well. However, true to their history, Dell executed this selling process very well and customers, finding it easy to use, have increased their purchases through the Dell website as a percentage of Dell's total sales.

Compare Dell's approach to the initial approach of the various airlines to the Internet. Did you try to use any of their sites in the late 1990s and the early part of the new millennium? Compared to some of the truly useful sites such as travelocity.com, the dedicated airline sites made it extremely difficult for you to buy from them the way you'd like to have bought. How much business did they lose from this non-user-focused approach to the Web? To their credit most of the dedicated airline sites are now much easier to use, tie to your frequent flyer account and help you manage your travel "your way."

Website user interface wasn't a problem for Dell. They've done an excellent job understanding the customer's interaction with the Internet and have constructed a website to facilitate that process. The result for Dell has been increased sales and a lower cost of selling.

Then there's amazon.com. No matter what, that is a strange name for a bookstore. Here's a business that used the Internet to create a whole new model for selling books. They sell strictly over the Internet and it works. Amazon.com has taken their demonstrated expertise at facilitating sales over the Web and built stores for others (ToysRUs and even another bookstore, Borders) as well as expanding the amazon.com "store" to include much more than books. And they are finally making a profit too.

[PART THREE]

THE EFFICIENCY SOLUTION

[THE EFFICIENCY SOLUTION]

(Part 3)

Then there's the magic of sales automation (known by the current buzz words "Customer Relationship Management"). The silver bullet to solve the sales problem. Who was that masked man who sold us that bill of goods?

Now, before you get me wrong, let me state unequivocally — customer relationship management software works — when it does. For those of you who have been in business for a long time, did automating the accounting process, in and of itself, make your business more profitable? Probably not. Automated manufacturing, again, in and of itself, probably didn't make your company more effective or more profitable either. However, to the extent that automation forced you to review and improve each process, you ended up with a better process and more efficient execution.

The challenge of automating sales is similar. Too many companies have looked to customer relationship management software as the holy grail, as the way to solve their fundamental sales problems. It isn't, and it won't.

This failure, or at least disappointment, is further compounded by the fact that when most companies finally decide to implement customer relationship management software, they're in too much of a hurry and just want to "get on with it." I mentioned earlier the importance of defining your sales process to allow you to make it more efficient. It's unlikely that you will be able to make something more efficient if you don't first understand what you're trying to do, and then how you're trying to do it.

The Trap in Small to Mid-Sized Companies

In small to mid-sized companies, the decision to switch to customer relationship management is usually delayed until something is very obviously wrong with sales results. And by then it's past time to act. The distressed management just wants to "pick a software package" and get it installed. A "thorough" investigation of what software their friends are using in their companies leads these now impatient managers to the likely selection of one of the more popular shrink-wrapped products: such as Act, Goldmine, Maximizer, SalesLogix or other equivalents.

Now, before I start my tirade, let me make this perfectly clear — these products are all potentially excellent choices for providing customer relationship management. The problem is — they are not necessarily the best for *your* company. These products are not interchangeable. In other words, just because one of these software packages works in a particular company, that doesn't mean it is the right one for your company. Each of these products has pluses and minuses depending on a particular company's needs.

Would you consider making an accounting or manufacturing software decision based primarily on what your friends are doing in their companies? No, you'd at least narrow down the advice you received to be coming from similar or identical companies. You intuitively understand that a solution that works for the finance or manufacturing needs of a custom sheet-metal fabricator may be entirely inappropriate for the needs of a swimming pool heater manufacturer. Somehow, when you make the mental switch to customer relationship management software, you throw that logic out the door. Is it because you don't understand the need to "manufacture" customers?

In our company's consulting practice I've seen too many cases of companies that hastily implemented an automated system. Later they discover it isn't used, doesn't work, or it becomes the excuse for almost everything that goes wrong in the sales or marketing area. How do you prevent this from happening to your company? Before I answer, let's take a look at the related problem that occurs in selecting customer relationship management software in a large company. Because, whether the company is large or small, the ultimate solution is the same, even though the process of what goes wrong is different.

The Large Company Has Its Own Difficulties

The missteps taken in selecting customer relationship management software for a large company can be the same ones found in the mid-size company, or the cause may be a different and equally deadly one.

In a large company, the selection of this software is finally deemed critical, and therefore assigned to a committee of people who have never been involved in the selection, implementation, or use of customer relationship management software. (To be fair, the use of customer relationship management software is a relatively new phenomenon, and therefore there aren't too many people who have been through the selection and installation before.) This notwithstanding, the large company almost always ensures additional problems by complicating the already difficult task the committee has before it. We usually find that the selection committee:

1. Has too much time — or too little

2. Is tasked to find the "best solution"

3. Is "fully represented" by all interested parties

4. Can't, won't, or doesn't map the sales process the company uses

And this means *what* exactly? Let's take a look at these issues one at a time.

1. *The committee has too much time — or too little.*

If the committee is given too much time it may never come to a conclusion. One of the risks in this selection process is fear of failure. The truth is, most customer relationship management projects fail. That is, in the best case, they don't meet expectations. In the worst case, the resulting system and software just aren't used at all. This increasingly well-known fact about selection failures gives rise to the need for the committee to study for as long as possible and to delay a decision until the "right one" can be found.

Here's a secret. No matter how much money you spend, there's no right solution. That doesn't mean there isn't a good one that works, just no *one* right solution. It's like linear programming, there are many possible right solutions; you're looking for *an* optimal one.

The "decisonus deferus" syndrome that often occurs in big companies compounds this problem. For example, let's see if Sally can defer this decision until someone else makes it. Then, if it's wrong, Sally can have plausible deniability. If it's right, well then Sally was on the committee that made an excellent decision.

The converse is also possible — too little time. In this case, the committee must solve the problem *now*. For whatever reasons the company waited too long and now a decision is required — immediately. The distressed management just wants to "pick a software package" and get it installed. This situation is akin to the problem found in small to mid-sized companies discussed above . . . and the solution process is similar, if not identical.

These other three team dynamics issues just further compound the difficulty.

2. *The committee is tasked to find the "best solution."*

Now what could be wrong with trying to find the best solution? For which problems? The customer relationship management process focuses on automating some or all of the so-called "marketing process." A detailed look at that process will come later, but for now assume that it includes traditional marketing and sales issues. This process is even more complex than the sales process discussed earlier, though they are obviously related.

Trying to find an automation solution for an ill-defined and complex process leads to numerous trade-offs. It can be very difficult, if not impossible, to determine what is important in this situation because you can't tell the difference between what you don't know and what you can't know. It is impractical, if not virtually impossible, to find a solution for an ill-defined process. When you add to that the increased process complexity involved with true customer relationship management, you further compound the problem. These trade-offs are difficult, and often make "best solution" a subjective and useless term. This being the case, the members of the committee will have difficulty agreeing on a "best solution."

3. *The committee is "fully represented" by all interested parties.*

Fat chance! If you've ever worked in a large company you know this is seldom true. The problem is further compounded by the fact that the most interested party is unlikely to be interested in spending any time on this project. Who's that? Salespeople.

For a customer relationship management system to work, it must be used. Sales is the most likely user. Countless real-world examples demonstrate that the most probable cause of failure in a customer relationship management system implementation is non-use (or at least irregular use) by the sales organization. Could it be that their lack of representation is reflected in their lack of use? If so, then why don't companies just make sure one or more sales people are on the committee?

Easier said than done. Sales people usually don't like serving on committees, if for no other reason than it can adversely impact their income. (If you're on a committee having meetings, it tends to get in the way of selling.) Even if you solved the earnings issue, sales people, by their nature, are often individuals who don't like serving on committees anyway. If the company uses field-based sales people, the problem is further compounded by the distance factor, because the rest of the committee is probably based at headquarters.

Given this dilemma, companies often substitute sales managers for sales people on the committee. This approach seems logical since these individuals (a) manage the sales people involved, and (b) were sales people themselves once. Even so, sales managers are not good substitutes because they just don't work the same way as sales people.

In most cases, sales managers are managers of sales people, and are no longer actively involved in managing their own accounts. To the extent they no longer deal with accounts on a primary basis, their credibility in describing what account-focused sales people will really do is suspect.

That's not to say their opinions are useless. But the management perspective just may taint their ideas. Their views reflect how a sales person should act, rather than how they, themselves, would act if they were still actively involved with selling. Bottom line, a sales manager on the committee is better than no sales representation. But, you need to make sure the manager you select for the team can help you understand how to design an automation process that focuses on what's in it for the sales person.

4. *The committee can't, won't, or just doesn't map the sales process the company uses.*

For lots of reasons, including several discussed above, the selection committee never gets around to understanding and mapping the process they are trying to automate. I know that sounds strange, but it is too true.

The task force assigned to examine the problem and offer a recommended solution often doesn't include process-oriented people as part of the team. Think about who would be most likely to represent your company (or did) in a customer relationship management software selection task force. Are any of them really process-oriented people? If not, then who is going to recommend that the process being automated first needs to be defined? Especially if the task force is already behind schedule.

An alternative solution is to simply have the committee get your existing sales process map from your sales manager. No problem there, right? In case your company is an exception to the rule, and you actually do have an existing sales process map, it is still necessary that the map be validated before it can be used.

Is It Hopeless?

So, how do you prevent or overcome these problems in small, mid-sized, or large companies? Hard as it may be to accept, you must quit looking for a quick, cheap fix. Quick fixes don't provide useful tools in management fads, and they don't work in customer relationship management software either.

Before you can automate, you must really understand the process you're trying to manage. It's very likely that the entire process is too complex for you to automate all of it initially anyway. Accept it. However, by understanding what you ultimately need to do, you can select a tool that may be of use to you longer term. It requires a lot of work to thoroughly understand the process you are trying to automate. It also requires that you truly comprehend the real secret to increasing sales. So let's get back to that.

[SECTION TWO]

THE SECRET . . . REVEALED

Secrets are things we give to others to keep for us.

Elbert Hubbard

The secret of a secret is to know when and how to tell it.

Anonymous

A secret is something that is not only told in strict confidence, but also repeated in strict confidence.

Anonymous

We dance round in a ring and suppose, But the Secret sits in the middle and knows.

Robert Frost

If you wish to preserve your secret, wrap it up in frankness.

Alexander Smith

Sometimes you just gotta trust that your secret's been kept long enough.

Anne Cammeron

If you want to keep something secret, don't write it down.

Richard Helms

I have not told half of what I saw.

Marco Polo

The secret of business is to know something that nobody else knows.

Aristotle Onassis

[EFFICIENCY'S NICE]

(But It's Really Not the Solution)

For now, that's enough on using efficiency methods to increase sales. This doesn't imply the ideas are a waste of time, because they aren't. Efficiency methods can give you a significant advantage in the marketplace. It's just that increased selling efficiency alone isn't the real breakthrough you need. The real breakthrough comes from understanding what the *right* thing to do really is. That is, how do you dramatically increase *effectiveness?*

In other words, how do you close the gap between top sales producers and the rest of the pack and thus improve the effectiveness, and therefore the performance, of your entire sales organization?

Before we took the sidecar down the efficiency path, I noted that companies have invested a "ton of bucks" in sales training and education without much to show for it in the way of results. It's time to figure out why! Could it be that selling is just too tough for most people? Or, does the sales profession just attract a high percentage of below average performers?

Some Hypotheses on the Cause of the Problem

In trying to answer this vexing performance improvement question, I considered and rejected several hypotheses. The following are some of those rejected possibilities.

1. *Most sales people are just fundamentally incapable of learning how to be great at selling.*

   Before you come completely unglued, I told you I rejected this hypothesis. However, you have to consider its potential validity. "Hmm, lots of training — no significant performance change. Given the many different instructors and different curriculum, which all resulted in no real improvement — maybe the students just can't learn."

   Well, as logical as this argument may be to some, it has no basis in actual practice. A cursory review of even a small number of sales people quickly reveals no correlation between sales ability and IQ. It's neither positively — nor negatively — correlated. Would that it were, because then we could just give sales people IQ tests and, based on the results, hire with confidence. Unfortunately, it's just not that simple.

Before we leave this premise, let me make clear that IQ is a relative subject. Some companies sell complex solutions that require a substantial technical or system understanding on the part of their sales people. The intelligence level necessary to understand these products or services can eliminate less knowledgeable people from the hiring process. However, within the group of people with sufficient education and intelligence to meet the minimum requirements of understanding, there's still no correlation — positive or negative — between relative intelligence and sales results.

2. *There's a holy grail to selling — it just hasn't been discovered.*

That's possible, but is it a practical solution? Maybe, despite the multitude of different methods, hundreds of years of applied experience, and more ways to close an order than anyone can remember, the "experts" just haven't found the holy grail of sales methods yet.

For this hypothesis to be useful you must consider how long selling had been going on. A *long time* — but "how long?" In fact, what was the *first recorded* sales transaction? It's easier to find than you might think. It's right there in Genesis 3:1-16. The snake sold Eve the apple. Yes, in spite of what you may have heard about another profession, sales is actually the "oldest profession."

Given this long historical record, I decided that it's not very practical for a company to wait for the discovery of the holy grail — or to take the time to find it themselves.

After discarding these two ideas, as well as others, what's left? What if it's not a *selling problem?* That's interesting. If it's not a selling problem — and sales people are not performing as well as they should — then whose problem is it? *It's a marketing problem!* — Say what? Is it a semantics problem? Well, actually, no.

With apologies to the academic community, sales is *not* part of marketing. Academicians describe the "marketing process" as the process that takes a company's mission, vision, values and capabilities and then maps them to a group of customers' needs, wants, expectations, and demands. This definition obviously includes sales. An excellent flow-chart representation of this process (developed by Dr. David R. Palmer of Santa Clara University) is included in Appendix A. However, because this entire complex process is often called the *marketing process*, too many people miss the unique role of *marketing* in this process and how it meshes with sales' role.

Marketing Versus The Marketing Process

While academicians have dubbed this marketing-to-sales process the "marketing process," it's a potentially deadly mistake to assume that sales is actually a part of marketing. Just because the process is called the "marketing process," doesn't imply that the marketing department should run it. I know this sounds confusing, that's part of how we got into this mess.

The marketing process, as defined, includes marketing *and* sales. A simple line drawing representing this process is shown in Figure 6. This line drawing cleverly reduces the excellent process diagram from Appendix A to a simple representation. After carefully reviewing the complete

process in Appendix A, or other variations of this marketing process, many people have asked the obvious question: If sales and marketing are two different functions
within this process, where does marketing stop and sales
begin?

The truth is, where that point exists *doesn't matter* —
except at the extremes of the process. There are a few
things Marketing must do, and some things that must be
done by Sales. Everything else, no matter what you want
to call it, including sales support, marketing communications, promotion, lead qualification, etc., can be done
under the auspices of either the marketing department or
the sales department in your company — provided
they're competent.

Figure 6.

If Marketing does these functions, they're called "marketing services" or "marketing communications." If they're done by Sales, they're called "sales support." It doesn't matter which department does it or what you call it, as long as it's done well. There is no evidence either from my personal experience or from research that indicates that either Marketing or Sales will be inherently better at managing these functions in any particular industry. It comes down to the skills of the individuals managing the functions and the process by which they are managed.

However, because of the confusing terminology used, it's too easy to forget to do marketing. But, you can't *forget* to sell. Without sales, the company folds pretty fast. Without marketing, sales becomes difficult, often impossible. Exactly what I mean by marketing will soon become clearer. The key issue is to not confuse the marketing *process* with marketing. Or worse, to confuse sales with marketing.

Try That Again

Notwithstanding all this confusing terminology, if Marketing doesn't do its job, Sales has to make up for it. It is a process, no matter what you call it. It starts with marketing and ends with sales. Referring back to Figure 6, work not done, or not done correctly, simply flows through the process to the right. Thus, defects that occur early in the process affect everything that is done afterward, including the ultimately unacceptable output.

Countless sales experts have tried to help sales people overcome a lack of marketing. They do this under many guises but the reality is they are trying to teach Sales to do Marketing's job. It doesn't work, it hasn't worked, and it won't work, at least not with enough sales people to make a significant difference.

Trying to teach sales people to make up for a lack of marketing is the wrong approach. The process just works much better with true marketing input. So, what do I mean by *marketing* input?

A Corollary

To understand the problem more fully, consider the design-to-production process as a corollary (see Figure 7). In that process, it's fairly clear that incomplete or poor design must be "made up for" by Production. If Design doesn't do its job, then the success of the company will depend on Production's ability to make up for this lack of design engineering.

Design	Hope for the best	Production

Figure 7.

Thirty years ago when production output was unacceptable in either quantity or quality, it was common practice for the CEO or division manager to call the production manager into his office to discuss this lack of performance. It never dawned on anyone (with the possible exception of Production) that the problem may have been "designed in." As silly as that seems today, that's the way it was. A reminder of this can be seen in a review of Deming's "red bead" experiment.[5]

In seminars in the 1970s and 1980s, Deming and his disciples would demonstrate a common fallacy of management using a variation of this red bead experiment. Deming would have an opaque jar of beads and would

---

5. For a more complete description of this experiment see *Out of Crisis* by W. Edwards Deming, MIT, 1982.

ask members of his audience to help him by producing white beads. Production consisted of reaching into the jar and removing a handful of beads. The "production worker" could not see into the jar, so production activity was simply to reach in and remove the beads.

Most of the beads in the jar were white, and some were red. The production workers' performances were measured by the percentage of white beads produced, with 100% being the goal. As you might expect, no amount of criticism, rewards, or "retraining" ever changed the results the "workers" achieved. Their individual production results varied within a statistically predictable range and were independent of any management interventions. It is obvious to all of us today that the percentage of red beads produced was predetermined by the "design" of the contents of the jar. This obvious (today) result was an eye-opener to management of that time.

As a result of this work by Deming and others, today, when there is a production problem, it is not uncommon to find both the production manager and the engineering/design manager in the CEO's office discussing solutions. In fact, management techniques such as design-for-production are commonplace today. Compare that to how most companies deal with a sales "production" problem.

Today, when your company has insufficient sales, who gets called into the CEO's office? Right, the sales manager. When was the last time marketing was asked to explain a lack of sales? OK, sometimes marketing support gets criticism, but recall that marketing support is not true "marketing" but rather an element in the marketing/sales process that can be managed by either the marketing or sales department.

The bottom line is that companies are still looking at the marketing-to-sales process through the same misguided eyes that were managing design-to-production processes 30–50 years ago. Companies learned years ago that trying to solve design problems in Production is a losing proposition.

Sometimes fixing the problem "downstream" works — sometimes it doesn't — and no matter what, it's unnecessarily expensive. The marketing-to-sales process presents the same dilemma. Whatever Marketing doesn't do, Sales must try to "make up for." And it may work, but probably not, and no matter what, it is unnecessarily expensive.

So What Is Marketing Supposed to Do?

Again, by "marketing" I am now talking only about the

very beginning of the process. And by "sales" I am referring to the very end of the process. It doesn't matter what
you call all the things that happen in the middle of the
process, such as merchandising, promotion, advertising,
PR, channel support, pricing and discount programs, etc.,
as long as they're well executed.

As was said earlier, when the marketing department
runs those functions, it is called marketing. When the
sales department runs these same functions, it is called
sales support. But, they need to be done well no matter
who runs them or what you call them. And, these functions usually aren't the *real* problem.

Not performing those functions at all often contributes
to a lack of sales or Sales inefficiency. However, not doing
the fundamental, critical, first job of marketing is the more
likely downfall of companies. Without doing the initial
work of marketing correctly, and then spending money on
the stuff in the middle of the process could, at best, be
wasting your money — or at worst, actually driving customers away.

Think about the manufacturing analogy again. Trying
to improve production output quantity or quality is limited by the quality of the design. We now know efforts to

improve output quality in Production are doomed to failure without working backwards in the process to find the root cause — which is often poor design. Such radical ideas as "design-for-manufactureability" came about during this learning process. The analog is absolutely true in the marketing-to-sales process.

So, to more fully understand the real role of marketing at the beginning of the process, consider where the highest failure rate occurs. There are three factors to completing the marketing-to-sales process. To successfully complete the process, you must understand:

Who buys?
Who, precisely, is your customer? If you are in the business-to-business marketplace, what kinds of companies are you targeting? What are their unique characteristics? How can you identify one when you see one? Who inside each of those companies is making, influencing, and championing the buying process and decisions?

Even in the so-called business-to-business marketplace the ultimate customer for what is being produced is usually a consumer. One thing you must keep in mind is how buying from your company will help your customer sell more to their customer.

If instead of business-to-business, you're selling to consumers either directly or through channels, who are these consumers? Who else, either as an influencer or decision maker, is involved in the buying process?

Your channel choice obviously affects this buying process. Agreeing to allow certain channel outlets to carry your goods affects *Who* can and will buy. Conversely, disallowing certain retailers or whole-salers to carry your line also has an impact on *Who* buys. Additionally, it is critical that you recognize that the channel is not your customer.

That does not suggest that the channel is not critical-ly important to your ability to reach the right *Who*. It's just that the channel is not *Who*. Too many manufac-turers make the mistake of thinking of the channel as the customer because that's who places the order and pays the invoice. Don't be confused. As is discussed below in *How* the customer wants to buy, the channel is a tool for you to use to help your customers and potential customers (your *Who*), buy the way they want to buy.

What are they buying?

It is very important to understand, from the customer's viewpoint, what each is trying to buy. This is not necessarily what you are selling — and in that difference is the opportunity — and the problem.

How do they want to buy it?

Too often sales people try to sell the customer rather than help them buy. It is critical that you understand the importance of matching your selling process with *How* the customer wants to buy. And, by the way, how often do you want to be *sold?*

As mentioned above, your channel can be an important part of your selling process when it is an important part of the customer's buying process. Selection of channel, whether wholesaler, retailer, or distributor should be done to allow the customer to buy the way he or she wants to buy. That is the real purpose of channel in the process. So called "channel conflict" occurs when manufacturers attempt to restrict how customers can buy or when manufacturers are influenced by their channel to avoid new outlets that are desired by the customer who wants to buy.

You see examples of "channel conflict" occurring regularly in the market and it has increased dramatically with the increased use of the World-Wide Web. Many short-sighted manufacturers and retailers are attempting to dictate *How* the customer can buy, rather than using the Web to facilitate the customer's ability to buy, buy more, and buy more often. Some examples include Levi Strauss, Macy's, and the bicycle industry.

In the year 2000, Levi Strauss launched and abandoned their Web-based, direct-to-consumer sales strategy. The hard cost was large and the "soft" costs are likely to be even greater as this once outstanding company continues to find new ways to alienate their market. The Levi strategy was flawed from the outset because it attempted to dictate *How*.

Consumers could buy Levi's directly from Levi Strauss via the Internet, or they could go into a retail store (so-called "brick and mortar") and buy Levi's, but they could not buy Levi's from a brick and mortar Web site (so-called "click and mortar"). Levi's retailers who had Web sites were not allowed to sell Levi's online.

Shortly after this strange strategy was launched, Levi announced that they were abandoning their strategy to sell Levi's direct to consumers on their site because they had found the cost per sale too high to support (and this was a surprise . . . to whom?). They now ask their retailers to support Web-based commerce.

If you consider that one of the reasons retail outlets exist is because the cost of serving an individual consumer is high and can't usually be covered by a single supplier of low cost goods, and you recognize that consumers are going to buy the way they want to buy, it seems clear that there was no hope for Levi's strategy. Given that credible people worked on the program, it would be interesting to see the internal documents (and related assumptions) that justified their approach. (For obvious reasons, Levi's is not making those documents publicly available.)

Let's consider Macy's. A few holiday seasons ago I decided to do ALL of my holiday shopping via the Internet. Two reasons: (1) I wanted to learn more about how the process worked, and (2) No time to shop. What an eye opener that experience was for me. But, to the point at hand, let me describe briefly my experience with Macys.com.

I chose to shop with them because I felt they would have a selection of items I was looking for and that by aggregating my order I could avoid buying a single gift whose shipping costs were significant compared to the price of the item. I also trusted that Macys.com would reflect merchandise and quality that I was familiar with (the *What* was known to me . . . or so I thought).

I found three items to purchase and placed my order. Fortunately Macys.com agreed to deliver prior to Christmas (I only had about a week . . . or less). However, the next day I got an e-mail from them saying that one of the items I wanted to buy was not available from Macys.com, but perhaps I could try either Macy's catalog or a Macy's store! My thought was probably the same as yours . . . and why don't YOU try the catalog and the stores, find it for me and ship it to me. If *How* I wanted to buy had included catalogs and stores I would have shopped that way. Besides, one of the reasons I selected Macys.com was a belief that they really were Macy's. Maybe not?

Lastly, let's take a quick look at the bicycle industry. Have you tried to buy a bicycle on the Internet? Maybe you haven't, but my research suggests that a lot of people would like to. The problem is, you really can't. Well that's not totally true. A very few bicycle lines are available on the Web that will refer you to a dealer,

Raleigh being the most notable with their Website bikeshop.com. Of course the only brand they offer is Raleigh.

But go to a much more complete site like bike.com and (as of this writing) you can't find very many bikes for sale. Wonder why? Channel conflict! The manufacturers claim their dealers will be very unhappy if their brands are sold on the Internet. Maybe so, but if that's *How* customers want to buy, somebody better figure out how to work a win-win scenario, or look for new brands without existing brick-and-mortar dealers to enter the market using the *How* of the Internet.

Further, could a well-trafficked site on the Internet drive sales for a network of dealers, thus creating "shelf-space" for a new brand of bike? When you try to tell the customer *How* they can buy, you run the risk that a competitor, who will sell *How* the customer wants to buy, will take advantage of your arrogance.

Marketing's Fundamental Job

Marketing's fundamental job is to understand *Who* and *What* and explain this to Sales — period. If this function is not done well, anything else which happens "downstream" in the marketing-to-sales process is going to be flawed. *Who* and *What* are the equivalent of the design step in the design-to-production process and, as we've learned, bad design results in unacceptable production. Before going into a further discussion of *Who* and *What*, you may be wondering about "why" people buy.

Why Not Why?

After first hearing or reading the *Who*, *What*, and *How* premise, some people suggest that the important question of "why" the customer buys has been omitted. There are two answers as to why I left out "why."

First, in many cases why doesn't matter. In truth the customers themselves often don't know "why." Second, and more important, why is really a part of *What* and *How*. As you'll see, if you truly understand *What* the customer is buying, and *How* they want to buy it, you'll come as close as is practical and useful to understanding why. This may not be a totally satisfying answer yet, but please stay with me and you'll see my reasoning unfold.

Say What?

Let's start with *What*. What is your customer really *buying* from you? Don't respond with what you sell. What is the customer *really* buying? That's simple you say — quality, service, support, or some other intangible. Can't fool you. Well, let's not get too smug.

In all my years of buying, selling, and managing, I've never ever encountered a company that said its products were poor quality and it provided bad service, but its prices were cheap. Have you? Everybody claims great quality and service. If a company's prices are lower, it just declares that the competition is charging too much, or that it is more efficient than the other suppliers are and it knows how to "keep its costs down."

OK, you say you really have quality and service and others don't. Where is your Olympic Gold Medal? Look, I'm not trying to be difficult, I'm just suggesting that it's more difficult to compete on "quality" and "service" generalities than you think. If you don't agree — ask your sales force.

That doesn't mean you can't compete on quality and service *specifics*. The bottom line is simple — what can a customer *really* buy from you that they *can't buy from anybody else*. Do you think you know? Good, stop reading and write it down. Now ask this same question of your Sales and Marketing people and see what answers they provide.

If You Know "What," Does Anybody Else?

If your company is really good, the range of answers by your internal people won't vary much to the question of *What* your customers buy. The critical question is: what does the sales department say? Or, better yet, how many different answers did you get from Sales?

Even if you assume a consistent answer from your Sales people, if they don't say the same thing the Marketing people said, then what? Can Sales sell what they answered for themselves? Can the company support that? Can Sales sell what the Marketing people said?

Look, if this were easy to do, your sales would be a lot higher than they are. If you think it is easy, maybe you're glossing over the problem, or you haven't asked your Sales people yet!

Diamonds Are Just Compressed Carbon

How about some examples of this *What* thing? Consider an easy one first: the diamond versus any other precious stone. Diamonds are substantially less rare than most other precious stones. For example, rubies are 45 times rarer. Look at the crown jewels in monarchs' crowns — very few diamonds.

Maybe they couldn't afford them? — I don't think so.

The reality is that until the early part of the 20th century, diamonds were a fairly common stone, and not considered overly valuable. Don't get me wrong, they weren't worthless, they just weren't rubies, emeralds or sapphires. Then about 70 years ago the diamond marketing cartel came up with the idea of describing what you could buy with a diamond, and therefore couldn't buy with any other stone.

A diamond is — forever. Don't get confused. Rubies don't wear out; they just didn't get to the "forever" position first. I think you'll agree that an effective ruby industry response to the "diamonds are forever" campaign couldn't very well be "us too."

So if diamonds are forever, for how long are the other precious stones? It doesn't matter — because it's not "forever." By that clever positioning of *What*, diamonds became "a girl's best friend" and the valuable "commodity" they are today.

The Model T Was a Car

What do you buy when you buy a car? It depends what you bought. Cars cost around $20,000 today. So if you spend $80,000 or more on what you drive, are you stupid? Not necessarily. Perhaps you didn't buy just a car.

If everybody wanted a commodity car, Henry Ford's Model T-200X would be all there is today. Alfred Sloan demonstrated, convincingly, that not everybody wanted to drive a commodity car. Today BMW, Mercedes, and Porsche (among others) give you a chance to buy the ultimate driving machine, a prestige automobile, or a toy. You have to want to buy a whole lot more than just a car if you're going to spend that kind of money.

There Are Cars and . . .

What's the difference between a high-end Infiniti and a high-end BMW, other than about $20,000? Decades of automobile excellence. The Ultimate Driving Machine. If all you want is a great "car" you don't need to spend that extra $20,000. And if you do, then you do.

In the early 1990s when Lexus and Infiniti first came to market, several dynamics merged to increase their sales significantly while simultaneously — and dramatically — reducing the sales of BMW and Mercedes.

1. Many BMW and Mercedes buyers of that time had only wanted a great car and couldn't buy one except from BMW and Mercedes. Remember what was going on in the late 1980s in terms of car quality and you'll understand.

    Cadillac had lost its mystique. People had gone from calling something the "Cadillac" of its class to considering how a Cimmaron could possibly be a Cadillac. On top of that, mainline Cadillacs had far too many defects for the buyer to feel they'd purchased a "Cadillac."

    Audi had come under attack as a vehicle that was manufactured with an "automatic acceleration" option — whether you wanted it or not. Fortunately this 'option' turned out never to have been included in the Audi. But that fact was not well known in the late 1980s, so most people shunned Audi as a possibility when considering a great car.

    Of course, the venerable Saab and Volvo were still available. And great cars they were, and are. However, many U.S. consumers find the design and amenities of a Swedish car to be mismatched to their needs. Saab and Volvo have steadfastly refused to change their Swedish models to better fit the U.S. market and in turn have suffered lower sales as a result. This scenario sounds a lot like the U.S. approach to the Japanese car market — and with similar results.

Bottom line, if you wanted a great car, your options were few and you could either compromise, do without, or overpay. If you bought a BMW, Mercedes, or one of their peers, you were acquiring more than a great car, and therefore you paid more. If all you really wanted was a great car, you paid for more than that — because these brands offered more.

2. Many people felt "guilty" for the excesses of the 1980s and decided to eschew the mantle of prestige.

3. The Lexus and Infiniti truly were (and are) great cars and some people wanted to try them.

The precipitous decline in sales of BMW and Mercedes caused observers at the time, who didn't understand the concept of *What,* to predict the demise of these two companies. BMW and Mercedes didn't fail — and not just because they were aggressive about adding lower priced cars to their lines. They didn't fail because *What* you can buy from Lexus and Infiniti is a subset of *What* you can buy from BMW and Mercedes.

The above description is probably best summed up by a quote from Patrick Shores of Atlanta, Georgia which was published in a 1994 edition of the *San Jose Mercury News*. The reporter wrote that Mr. Shores had just finished trading in his three-year-old Lexus and was replacing it with a new Mercedes rather than another Lexus. The Mercedes he selected cost $20,000 more than a new Lexus. Mr. Shores is quoted as stating, "The Lexus was one of the most enjoyable cars I have ever owned...," and that the Lexus dealer had provided "...unmatched service." So why then did he spend $20,000 more for a Mercedes? "... [P]eople look at you differently when you drive a Mercedes," he said. He certainly knew *What* he wanted to buy.

We Sell Commodities

OK, some skeptics say differentiation works easily with diamonds and BMWs, but what if you're in the commodity business. Consider Frank Perdue. Frank sold dead chickens — at a premium price. He just had to understand what *his* customers wanted to buy that they couldn't buy from others — consistent quality each time, and a yellow color.

Frank moved his Perdue brand out of the price-driven commodity market by understanding that many customers wanted to buy something no one else offered. He recognized that chicken quality varied too much within a brand to give consumers any confidence that they knew *What* they were buying. Frank fixed that with a policy and system that provided a consistent product — package to package — day in and day out. He also realized that along with consistency, many customers would pay for better quality — whatever that was.

With a little research on his part, he came to understand how customers graded chicken. He discovered that customers in his market area believed that the more yellow the skin color, the higher the quality of the chicken. Frank needed a natural solution to this preference since chemicals or dyes weren't acceptable. He discovered Marigolds. By feeding his chickens Marigold flowers, he could positively affect the 'yellowness' of their skin color. By truly understanding *What* and finding a way to execute, Frank elevated a commodity product, chicken, to a value-added product, Perdue Chicken.

Then there's the ultimate commodity — dirt. One of the 1993 Malcolm Baldridge Awards was given to Granite Rock, a Watsonville, California sand and gravel supplier. What's so special about Granite Rock's dirt that they receive a 6% average price premium from their customers for their sand and gravel? Better dirt? Get outta here! It's just dirt.

However, for their customers who want to buy it, Granite Rock provides dirt on time, as agreed, when, where, and exactly how the customer wants it — every time. Other suppliers sell to customers who just want dirt, or who don't require the "extra" services that Granite Rock supplies. Nobody has a monopoly. Customers buy what they want from the supplier who provides it.

If nobody supplies what a group of customers want, then those customers do without — and they usually complain about price — until somebody figures out how to profitably meet their needs. *It's only a commodity if you look at what you're selling, instead of what the customer is buying.*

Can It

Consider a recent situation from two perspectives to gain additional insight into *What*. In the early 2000s, the aluminum can industry was facing a sales crisis the likes of which they hadn't seen in a very long time. As you may not know, in the last 20 years aluminum cans have become the dominant beverage container in an $11 billion market. How did they get to that position?

Simple. Containers are basically a commodity. After all, the consumer is buying the beverage inside. This implies that the container with the lowest total cost that accomplishes the required tasks wins, hence aluminum's dominance. Let's see why.

Aluminum has several benefits over alternative containers:

1. Glass breaks

2. Plastic containers permit oxygen to enter the container (plastic is permeable by oxygen). This means that carbonated beverages go 'flat' faster in a plastic container

3. Plastic containers have a tendency to tip over on the production line

4. Plastic containers fill slower on a production line

These are all very good reasons for the beverage man-ufacturer to prefer aluminum as a commodity container. Aluminum is cheaper, faster and easier to ship. It there-fore adds very little cost, and since containers have his-torically provided no real value-added — at least to the ultimate consumer — price and ease of use to the bever-age supplier has been the key to gaining market-share.

Now if you're a plastic or glass container company this situation isn't good. You've watched your glass market-share shrink over the years and plastic has never really reached its potential. So what do you do?

What if you change the rules of the game? What if the container were no longer a commodity? (Here's a perfect example of a business-to-business opportunity being turned on its head by thinking about the ultimate end-consumer.) What if packaging (i.e. the container) became a differentiator? Could you create a valuable container in glass or plastic that couldn't be easily replicated by alu-minum? You betcha.

That's exactly what's happened. Have you been in a gro-cery store or liquor store lately? Get a load of the "cans." The container, be it plastic, glass, or aluminum, is becoming an integral part of the brand positioning. (Maybe there was a clue here all along. After all, in many parts of the country a liquor store is called a "package store.")

The famous Coke glass bottle shape is now available in plastic. AriZona Beverages has developed a new sports bottle-shaped plastic container for their teas. According to an article in the October 6, 1997 issue of *Business Week*, the beverage will retail for $1.50 and the container will cost 28¢ — more than the cost of the liquid inside. *What* is the consumer really buying?

By helping beverage companies provide additional differentiation of their products, (by thinking about the customer's customer) the non-aluminum container companies have helped themselves compete with the more efficient aluminum container. As Harold Laski once said "When the rules of the game prove unsuitable for victory, the gentlemen of England change the rules of the game." Understand *What* your customers — and their customers — could buy, and you too, can change the rules of the game.

Infotech and the Paradigm Shift

An interesting phenomenon in the marketplace today is the loss of what used to be the apparently sustainable competitive advantage large companies such as AT&T, Sears, Digital Equipment, Silicon Graphics, Kodak, and IBM once had. It may appear that these companies are losing their dominant market position because they lost their competitive advantage in the market.

Baloney! They just quit thinking like a customer and started expecting the customer to think like them. If you look at *What* the customer is buying, in many cases it hasn't changed, with the possible exception of IBM, which I'll get to shortly.

AT&T provided *reliable* long-distance service. Now that has become commonly available through other sources and yet AT&T charges for it as if it were a premium product. *What* is being provided? MCI, Sprint and others can now provide the same *What*. Why should anyone pay AT&T more? For AT&T to continue to succeed in long distance, they need to find another *What* since their previous differentiator is recognizably no longer valid.

Sears lost its way. They quit understanding *What* customers were buying from them, and Wal-Mart took their place — and did it for the 1990s. It's tough to see the real world from the top of one of the world's tallest buildings. However, if you really look at the two stores and *Who* they served at their peak, you'll find more similarities than you might expect. Wal-Mart simply became the Sears of the 1990s because Sears abandoned ship.

In their zeal to find a new *What*, Sears has tried several ill-fated solutions including the silly attempt at a "softer side." Sources even told me that Sears was planning their own line of ladies' perfume. Do you know a female who would consider buying it? One male member of one of my audiences asked if they were going to call it "Craftsman?" Recently, Sears has rediscovered their roots and appears to be refocusing on the hard goods side of their business. Time will tell if they are able to reestablish a useful *What* for a group of *Who* that care.

Digital Equipment (DEC) provided department-level computing. The personal computer industry took the same *What* — computing that is decentralized — and moved it further. DEC should have recognized that the *What* their customers were buying wasn't changing, just how it could be delivered. Instead they looked at what they were selling instead of *What* the customer was buying. They should own the workstation and PC market today — at least at the corporate level. They don't because Founder/CEO Ken Olsen made a conscious — and mistaken — decision.

What's even stranger about that scenario is that one of the most profitable segments of the PC market is the server portion. Compaq Computer, which purchased DEC, tried to claim a solid position in this server market. Given that a server is just a modified minicomputer, you'd think that the DEC brand would have been valuable to Compaq to help penetrate this market. Apparently not, since the brand was never used.

Silicon Graphics (SGI), as an early draft of this book was being written, laid off a substantial number of people and fired their president. How'd that happen to a company that just six months before was a high flyer? They failed to recognize *What* many of their customers were really buying. Sure, some people are buying access to the latest, state-of-the-art graphics modeling tools. But many others are just buying "very good." Advances in technology now allow "very good" to be purchased for a lot less money than SGI wants for their "best." Look at *What* your customer base is really buying and then find the best way to deliver it — or the market will spend its money elsewhere.

Kodak's customers buy memories. Those memories might best be captured digitally these days. The *What* hasn't changed, but how it's delivered has. Can Kodak find a profitable way to adjust? Why not, somebody will. The problem for Kodak is that their profits may be a lot less than they once were. They're better off accepting this value equation change than stubbornly focusing on how great it used to be — on their way out of business.

Then there's IBM. Now here's a case where the *What* probably really did change. In the early days of computers, the *What* you bought from IBM was job security. Think about it. The MIS manager of the 1950s, 1960s, and even much of the 1970s, didn't really know anything about computers. They ran finance and accounting and since they were going to be the major user of computers, they were elected to manage the computer department.

IBM sales and technical support people made sure that these new 'experts' appeared to be so to their bosses. This approach worked for years. Then two shifts came together that caught IBM off guard. The new generation of MIS professionals didn't need the IBM expertise, and computing platforms changed. The *What* that IBM's customers were now buying changed and IBM neglected, prior to CEO Lou Gerstner, to change with it.

In fact, one of the keys to Mr. Gerstner's success was his ability to refocus the company on the customer. For too long, senior management at IBM had become isolated from the market. They had made the dangerous decision that they understood the market, or worse, could influence the ultimate direction of the market based on their superior knowledge of what customers *should* need, want, and demand. Funny thing about customers — they tend to spend their money as they see fit, whether you like it or not.

Assume a Position

The whole process of positioning, a termed coined by Al Ries and Jack Trout over 25 years ago, requires that you understand *What* the customer is buying. Pre-dating positioning is Rosser Reeves' Unique Selling Proposition (USP). Again, this is another way of describing the *What*. However, to apply either positioning or USP correctly, you look from the customers' viewpoint. That is, *What* are *they* buying — not what are *you* selling.

Well-positioned products or services take advantage of this understanding. You can't effectively position a product or service without a thorough understanding of what the customer can buy from you that they can't buy elsewhere. Because, as Ries and Trout point out, you don't position a product, you position the prospect or customer's mind. Or, as Jeff Krawitz, a marketing professor at Columbia University Graduate School of Business puts it, "The ultimate result of the total marketing effort is the position created in the target customer's mind." And, by the way, it is much easier to take advantage of ideas that are already in those minds than to try to change those minds.

Once again, it becomes critical for you to understand this *What* from the *customers'* perspective. How can you get that perspective? The obvious answer is to talk to customers. Easier said than done. While you do need to get out more (more on this starting on page 123), your first try at understanding the customers' view of *What*, is best discovered with a survey.

I recommend the following type of survey, done by an outside, professional firm. The "truth" you need in this initial process is difficult to gather on your own for a couple of reasons:

1. The customer is less likely to tell you the whole truth

2. Even if they do, you may know too much, and you are

likely to say at some point to the person being interviewed, "yeah, but . . ." — because they are "wrong", and once you do that, the interview is over

So, how should the survey discover this *What*? First, you need to survey three categories of "customers":

1. Those who buy from you today

2. Those who used to buy from you and don't anymore, but still buy something similar

3. Those who've never bought from you before, but appear to buy something similar

By interviewing these three categories of customers, you learn the real difference between you and your so-called competitors. You see, your current customers, at least those who are happy, usually can describe *What* they're buying from you.

Your former customers left for a reason — right or wrong. *What* did they want to buy they couldn't buy from you? Did they find it? By talking with former customers you gain a better understanding of how you are truly different from other solutions on the market.

Your "not yet" customers are shopping elsewhere for a good reason; they want to buy something you don't provide. Or, they buy from others for a bad reason; they want *What* you provide, and don't know you provide it.

If they don't want *What* you provide, they are correct in not buying from you. If they don't know *What* you provide, and if they did they would want to buy it, then the question is why are they misinformed? It could be because they have not seen or heard your message and just don't know about you. If this is the case, more advertising and promotion could lead to increased sales. If, on the other hand, they have seen your advertising and promotion and have been misled by it to believe incorrectly about your company, more advertising will have a negative effect on sales.

Aside from helping you to further understand your valuable difference in the market, this third, not-yet, group can help you to know what, if anything, to do more or differently with your advertising and promotion spending. If most of the people who don't buy from you, don't for the right reasons, more advertising probably won't fix it.

How can you use all of the survey knowledge provided by these three groups to help you effectively position your company in their minds? Obviously, once you clearly understand this *What*, you need to come up with a concise way of stating it. You need the so-called elevator conversation — that's what you say on an elevator to someone riding with you about your business in that short amount of time.

This so-called elevator conversation is a longer version of your positioning statement which is further reduced to your USP. It's all basically the same thing just repackaged. My way of packaging the idea is to ask you to understand *What* customers are actually buying from you.

Additionally, if you've done the survey well, you'll also know to what extent you should go after new customers who may be inadvertently buying "wrong."

Bottom line, find out *What* from your customers' perspective before you attempt to create your USP or positioning statement.

Branding

Branding is another marketing tool that has regained popularity. There are numerous useful definitions of

Branding. One that I like is from Lynn Upshaw. Branding is, " . . . an assortment of expectations established by the seller that, once fulfilled, forms a covenant with its buyers." Said my way, "a Brand is a short-hand trigger for the positioning in the buyer's mind to remind them of *What* they get from buying this product or service."

During the recession in the late 1980s and early 1990s, and virtually all recessions prior, Brands appeared to fall out of favor, as much of the buying public appears to prefer private label. Is this really the case? Does the consumer really prefer private label? It depends *What* the customer is buying.

Strong brand identity helps the customer understand quickly the *What* they can confidently know they're buying. Perdue branded his chicken by understanding *What* his customers wanted to buy (consistently tender, flavorful chicken). Windows are branded (Pella, Anderson), as are other mundane items including water. Even simple products like tap water can be branded (Aquafina).

Strong brand identity can be established in various ways. Sprint's *What* when they first entered the long distance market was call clarity. They developed the first fiber-optic cable network and used call clarity as their differentiator. They symbolized this benefit with the long-running campaign that stated that you could hear the sound of a pin drop over their ultra-clear lines. To this day, Sprint still features the "pin drop" in their commercials and messages. Just as rubies last as long as diamonds, AT&T and MCI lines are just as "clear" as Sprint, but Sprint holds the clarity position which has been reinforced with the pin drop identifier.

Branding of consumer products is commonplace. Branding of industrial products is also more common than you might think. AMP connectors is a very strong brand within the electronics industry. In more recent years the high technology industry has discovered marketing — at least the promotion side of the process — and has begun to apply what might be considered consumer marketing to some of their products.

The most notable is the Intel Inside campaign from Intel Corporation. For these campaigns to have any real effect on anything other than the advertising agency's bottom line, somebody must think through *What* the customer is buying, and make sure the advertisements send that message. The issue here is understanding the so-called value-chain. That is, who is the ultimate buyer of the Branded product? Intel's microprocessors have no intrinsic value until they are included in a complete product. For the Intel Inside ingredient branding concept to provide true Brand value, it must ultimately have some positive affect on the final buyer's behavior.

Some industrial marketers mistakenly believe that a unique name and logo are all it takes to create an industrial Brand. In the best case, this approach may make it easier for the buyer to remember your product — but not necessarily your Brand. In the worse case, this may just be an expensive exercise in ego gratification. It is possible, however, that creation of an apparent industrial Brand could have a positive effect on your stock price, and that may be very worthwhile. Just remember that if you go down that path, you will be forced to continue spending on this alleged branding program, whether it is providing true Brand value or not — or your stock price will suffer.

One thing all great Brands have in common — both consumer and industrial — is a consistent look and feel. This is obvious to most of us in consumer Brands, but it is equally true for industrial Brands. Consider Snap-On Tools. Everything about the company exudes consistency

— right down to their trucks. For a hybrid example consider the Caterpillar Brand.

Caterpillar or CAT and its ubiquitous yellow earthmoving and farm equipment is a highly identifiable Brand. Even for those of us who have never, and will never, purchase or use this equipment, the Brand signifies power and quality in big equipment. Can those attributes be moved to other goods? Positioning gurus Ries and Trout caution against virtually any type of line-extension based on the proven probable outcome of decreased Brand value.

They describe inside-out thinking as the disease that permits marketers to try to transfer generalized attributes of "goodness" to line-extensions. Ries and Trout together and separately correctly recognize that this backward thinking fails to understand *What* the customer is really buying and *What* the Brand is actually triggering in the buyer's mind. The line extension strategy ultimately fails and damages the entire Brand because the trigger doesn't tie to any *What* anymore.

So how did the CAT brand successfully end up on footwear? Well, it took several tries to get it right and, I argue that CAT footwear is not a Brand but rather a logo. There are some Brands that reach a point where they have a "life" of their own and can become a logo. Two Brands that come to mind in this category are Disney and Harley-Davidson. CAT is attempting to do the same thing.

In their latest attempt to move the CAT Brand to logo status in footwear (the first tries at this failed because CAT misunderstood how logoing actually works), they have finally understood that, at least initially, the logo must be applied to CAT-credible products. Therefore, they have correctly required that for the shoe line to bear their logo, it must "feel" like a CAT. Next time you are anywhere near a store where Gen Xers or Gen Y kids shop, take a look at the CAT shoes. If ever a shoe could look like a CAT, these do.

While some Brands can transcend the complex utility of mind trigger and shortcut to *What*, first and foremost, successful Branding takes an understanding of *What* your ultimate customer needs, wants, and demands to buy from your Brand: What is it they can't buy anywhere else? Then it requires a commitment of time and dedication to follow it through. Money is nice, but not critical. Many a great brand has established popularity via word of mouth. In fact, as too many former dotcoms learned in the last quarter of 1999, money alone can't create a

Brand. (As a former co-worker used to say, "Nine women can't have a baby in one month.")

Why Oh Why?

Recall that on page 92, I told you that "why" wasn't important. I suggested that why was really *What* and *How* in disguise — or *What* and *How* said another way. If you look at the above examples (and others you may think of), you'll notice why the customer is buying. It's because they need, want, or demand the *What* that company uniquely provides and they can acquire it *How* they want to buy it.

Why do they need, want, or demand it? Who really knows?

Does it matter? Maybe.

Can you find out? With some work.

Will the work payoff? It depends.

You see, sometimes even the customer doesn't really know why. But they almost always know *What* and *How*. Having said all that, the value is in knowing what these customers have in common. That can help you identify the other critical factor — *Who* buys.

Who's On First?

Of course, for an advertisement or other promotional activity to be effective, you must also understand with whom you are trying to communicate. So, let's take a look at *Who*.

Who is actually buying your products or services? Is it the user? Not always. In the business-to-business market, the *Who* could be several people playing various roles in the buying process. Truly understanding *Who* is buying helps to focus Sales on the right targets. If you don't help sales people understand *Who* to sell to, they will try to sell to whomever they find interesting. That may or may not be the right target for your company.

Almost every company I've worked with has horror stories of Sales bringing in opportunities that don't fit the company's skill set or preferred offering. But Sales points out that if the product could just be changed "a little bit," the sale would be easy. You've probably heard that one too many times yourself. If your sales organization keeps bringing you new prospects that don't want *What* you've got, but will buy with a modification, then I submit you have one of three possible problems.

1. Sales doesn't understand *What* you offer

2. Sales isn't focused on the right *Who*

3. Your offering to the market is insufficient

Obviously sales people try to convince you that the answer is #3. Do you know which answer is correct in your case?

Underwear

For many years, Jim Palmer was the corporate spokesperson for Jockey brand underwear for men. The picture of him wearing Jockey underwear appeared on billboards across the country. He helped increase sales of Jockey underwear. Why?

How does a picture of Jim Palmer in underwear motivate men to go out and buy underwear? It doesn't. Nor was it supposed to! You see, over 70% of men's underwear are bought by women, for the men in their lives. The marketing professionals at Jockey were focused on *Who* buys — *not* the user.

Pasta Deluxe

Would you pay $9.00 a pound for pasta in a bag? (Just in case you're thinking about the answer, Ronzoni pasta in the supermarket goes for about 89¢ a pound.) So, how is John and Carey Aron's Pasta Shoppe succeeding with pasta priced at about $9.00 per pound. Simple — now that they did it.

The Pasta Shoppe produces over 150 different and unique pasta shapes for specific events. They have $-sign pasta for a "thank you" gift, Star-of-David shapes for bar mitzvahs, houses and hearts for house-warming parties, and, coming soon, NFL logo-shaped pasta. Don't tell me that the citizens of Green Bay, Wisconsin; Dallas, Texas; and Oakland, California; at least, won't buy this stuff by the truck-load. Can cartoon characters be far behind?

The Arons took a commodity product, added a twist, and focused on various *Whos* that would want the unique *What* they created. Their products are also bought by the Philadelphia Museum of Art, BankAmerica, Fieldcrest, and others as corporate gifts. Now that they did the obvious, other target *Whos* are all over the place.

The Complex World of Business-to-Business

In many complex business-to-business sales there are several people involved in the buying process. So who's the customer? Potentially all of them. And, to further complicate the matter, they may not all be buying precisely the same *What*.

So, how do you figure this out? There's only one way. You have to spend time in the marketplace. Great marketers, whether they are the CEO of a small or mid-sized company, or a full-time strategic or product marketing professional in a larger company, must get out from behind their desks and spend time in the market. The spy novel author, John Le Carré said, "...a desk is a dangerous place from which to view the world." He's absolutely right.

You Need to Get Out More

In the formative years of a company the president/CEO spends a substantial portion of his or her time with customers. New presidents, division managers, and marketing professionals often do the same thing. This allows them to validate and understand their capacity to "think like a customer," to borrow a phrase from Harvard Business School's, Rosabeth Moss Kanter. The problem is that this "affliction" (the need to spend time with customers) eventually wears off, and their time in the marketplace diminishes — often to zero.

This is a doubly dangerous situation. First, they lose contact with the market, and second — and possibly worse — they still believe they think like a customer. In reality they now hope the customer thinks like them!

You say your company's too big for you to spend substantial time in the marketplace anymore. Well, I tell you what then, stay in the office. If your company's like most, and you isolate yourself long enough, the company will eventually become a size that's small enough for you to go out and visit customers again. In fact, in order to survive, you'll probably have to.

Look at what happened to IBM. In its early days Tom Watson Sr. personally stayed close to customers, and instilled a culture within the company that insured that all senior managers did likewise. When Tom Watson Jr. took over from his father, that mind-set continued. Somewhere along the line that thinking-process got lost. IBM got too big to need to listen to customers and ultimately under John Akers' tenure that disconnect came home to roost in the form of performance that could no longer be tolerated.

What did Lou Gerstner, an executive with virtually no experience in the computer or related industries, do first? Simple, he spent time with customers and insisted that his senior mangers return to this practice. The results speak for themselves.

Sam Walton built a $55 billion retail business in the last half of his lifetime. He did it one store at a time and he spent virtually every day in those stores until the day he died. Five days a week Sam visited stores. He knew that's where the money came from. He hired others to handle the major portion of the "internal stuff," the stuff that's got most CEOs bogged down so they can't get out of their offices. Sam kept his priorities focused on the only asset that matters: Customers *Who* can buy *What* they want — from you.

Before you say, "Sure, that's easy for a retailer, he just goes out on the floor," let me say, "Don't go there." If you want to make excuses for not visiting customers, go ahead, but it won't change the resulting damage. But, just to be fair consider Michael Dell again.

Here's a "kid" who started a "mail-order" computer business from his dorm room and built it into the number-one personal computer company. He sells "mail order" for goodness sake. Guess what, at over $35 billion in sales, Michael still spends a substantial portion of his time visiting customers. Dell is out-running and out-gunning the other personal computer companies, and has IBM, Hewlett-Packard, Compaq and others nervous. The real reason for Dell's success has a whole lot to do with Michael's larger commitment to personally staying in touch with the market. He's far more personally in touch with his customers than the top executives of those other companies.

A few years ago, Apple Computer "targeted" Dell. Steve Jobs at an Apple press conference in November, 1997, talked about new Apple products, new sales channels (direct to the customer, made to order via the Internet), and new manufacturing systems. Sounds great — sounds like Dell, with two differences. First, Apple has the Apple operating system used by maybe 5% of the personal computer market; Dell supports an operating system used by over 80% of the market. Apple has a better operating system if you "think different[ly]." This might be true, but the marketplace keeps voting "differently."

The second difference is the degree of commitment to understand the market. Steve Jobs helped pioneer the personal computer market. When he was hungry he understood how to think like a customer. Today he suggests that the customer should think like he does. Compare that approach to Michael's spending time with customers to understand how they think. Steve Jobs is undoubtedly a talented individual, and many of his ideas have resonated well with consumers, but that doesn't give him the right to tell customers how they should think. The marketplace votes with its wallet. While Apple is clearly back from the dead, time will tell how customers vote on Steve's suggestion that they think "his way."

Along with other developments, Dell has pioneered processes to reduce the cost of distributing personal computers. So? The real breakthrough came from understanding what processes could be streamlined while adding value for the customer and simultaneously reducing costs. These ideas came from the market — not from an internal, navel-staring session.

The one secret great companies share is a true understanding of *Who* buys and *What* they're buying. You won't find those answers in your office. They only come from your personal and continuing interaction with the market.

In 1982, Tom Peters and Bob Waterman wrote a best selling book entitled *In Search of Excellence*. As consultant observers, they attempted to explain the characteristics that were intrinsic to great companies. Looking back on this list of so-called great companies, we find today that of those listed, some are still considered great, a few are out of business and the rest are back with the pack. Did these companies change how they operated, or perhaps, did Peters and Waterman, as so many others since then, simply fail to find the "right" criteria for selecting greatness?

After spending over 17 years in industry, I finally became a consultant. So now perhaps I'm qualified to give you my two-cents on the "secret" to becoming and remaining a great company. Even if I'm not qualified, here it is.

In consistently great companies the CEO or division general manager spends a substantial portion of his or her time with customers in their environment. The CEO or division general manager really can "think like a customer" because they see and talk to them regularly. The importance of this understanding is then diffused throughout the company.

This may not be all you need to do, but it makes a huge difference and makes up for a lot of other shortcomings. Take the challenge. If you're the CEO or general manager, spend at least 25% of your time in the marketplace over the next twelve months. See if you don't find what countless CEOs and general managers I've spoken to have discovered.

After that first year, most of them report to me that the *only* change they intend to make in the next year is to spend more time in the market. As they used to say at Nike, "Just do it." And, to paraphrase Nike's new slogan, You Can! It works.

Knowing *Who* and *What* Is the Difference

What does all this lead to? Without knowing *Who* and *What*, the Production side of your process (Sales) can't be expected to produce as well as it could. If you want to improve the overall performance of your sales organization you need to spend less time on *How* training, and more time on helping sales people understand *Who* and *What*. My point is simple:

The real reason more sales people aren't great is because most of them don't know *What* **and/or** *Who* **and they don't get it figured out.** The really top sales producers aren't materially better at *How* to sell; they've just found a *Who* and *What* that works for them.

To demonstrate this further look at a couple of classic sales problems and evaluate the *How* solution versus the *What* solution.

Some Classic "Sales" Problems

Your company's products are the "best in the industry," yet you consistently lose sales to competitors with broader product lines. You may eventually add products to your line, but cash flow requirements dictate that sales of the current products need to increase. How can you get Sales to stop losing business to the competition?

To overcome this problem sales managers usually exhort their sales people to:

1. Focus on what you do have, not what you don't have. The products you have are great; dwelling on what's missing just gets you down and makes selling tougher

2. Believe in yourself. Listen to motivational tapes — stay pumped

3. Figure out for yourself what the attributes of your incomplete line are. After all, the company introduced this line on purpose. You should be able to determine the benefits of your company's incomplete line. Just think about it. If that doesn't work — think harder.

4. By all means, don't blame "management"

Pardon me, but what a crock! It's very simple. The company introduced a partial product line for a reason. Maybe they didn't think a complete line was necessary at all. Or, perhaps not for everyone. Great, maybe they're right. But Marketing's fundamental job is to understand to whom this partial product line is valuable and *What* they'll find valuable. Then Marketing communicates that information and insight to Sales.

If it turns out there aren't enough customers to meet the sales revenue targets, then Marketing must develop a compelling understanding of *What* could be interesting to more target customers. Positive thinking on the part of Sales is not the solution. **Getting Marketing people into the field to discover the solution is the answer**.

THE SECRET TO SELLING MORE

This situation is again analogous to trying to get Production people to solve a Design problem. They may — if you're lucky. But why would you expect them to be able to? The solution is to get the Design experts back involved to understand what the design flaw is, and how to correct it — quickly. That's Design's job. We know it in the product manufacturing process, it is equally true in the marketing/sales process. If a partial product offering was a mistake, then Marketing needs to own up to the problem.

Let's look at another example. In this case the company has been experiencing an excellent sales history which includes increased sales and good margins. "Suddenly" a competitor introduces an expanded and improved product line that is enticing many current customers to switch, or at least to seriously consider switching.

Again, Sales management will focus on cajoling the sales force to:

1. Study the competition and find its weaknesses

2. Act on those weaknesses by featuring them in future sales presentations without "knocking the competition"

Is this a productive use of Sales people's time? According to the 28th edition of the *Dartnell Sales Force Compensation*

Survey (1994-1995), field sales people spent an average of 13.9 hours of an average 46.5-hour work week face-to-face with customers. That's about 25% of their time. Now, let's make them even more inefficient by tying them up developing a competitive analysis. Who conned management into putting all this on Sales? What a great deal for Marketing — and what a bad deal for the company.

I discussed earlier that the proper role of field sales was to provide value to the customer at the customer's site. Sales people need to be focused on spending their time doing that — and they should be given the information and tools necessary to do it.

What is the real problem? First, why was the company surprised by the competitor's introductions? Where was Marketing while this was going on? OK, sometimes we all get surprised. That's reasonable. But, then, why doesn't Marketing jump into the fray and determine how the competitor's new offering affects the customers' perceptions of their company's position? In other words, how does this new competition affect *What* the customer can buy and *Who* cares?

Now before you say, "Well, we just want the Sales force to gather this information so Marketing can analyze it and determine the solution," let me say, "That's not how it usually works." Sales people are not consistently accurate reporters of customer's needs, wants, and demands. Sales people have their own biases. To the extent Marketing relies on Sales' input exclusively for their market understanding, they are very likely to be misled. Besides, most marketing people spend too much time behind their desks looking at the results of simulated markets (i.e. tests), rather than being out in the real world. If you have a surprise attack from the competition, everyone, including Marketing, needs to get into the trenches. While you could argue that this is not a Sales problem, it could become a sales problem if the company doesn't act to solve it.

The Secret (In Case You Missed It)

If I haven't made it clear to this point (or if you just skipped ahead to this point) here's the bottom line:

If you want your sales organization to really be able to provide "value-added" selling, "consultative" selling, or some other non-price driven sales process, then Sales needs to understand *What* your firm offers that can't be bought elsewhere, and **Who** wants to buy that. *This is Marketing's unique purpose in life.* Marketing has to figure this out and teach it to Sales.

The real difference between top producers in a sales organization today and the rest of the pack is their ability to figure out for themselves what the marketing organization has neglected to find out. Marketing's number one job is understanding **Who** buys and **What** they're really buying. *You can reduce the gap between the good and the great performers in your sales force if you quit relying on each sales person's ability to figure this out, and have Marketing do it for them.*

Sales training classes *should* start out with Marketing providing an explanation of the *What* and the *Who.* Unfortunately most of these training programs skip over this critical issue and just talk about *How.*

How is no longer the problem in most sales organizations. Or if it is, teaching people *How* to sell is reasonably well understood. If your hiring process and subsequent training programs can't solve the *How* problem for you, there are hundreds of books and training programs that can help you.

The newer, and I think better, programs try to have the trainees determine the *What*. The problem with this approach is that no one in class, usually least of all the trainer, really knows if any of these *Whats* are legitimate, unique differentiators in the market. If you're conducting training classes, or sending your sales people to training classes where they are expected to come up with a unique selling proposition, or equivalent, you're making a big mistake. It isn't going to happen. ***That's the whole problem.***

Sales training programs that begin with an attempt by Sales to determine *What* and *Who* indicate that no fundamental marketing has been done in the company. Why not? Who abdicated this responsibility, and how did they get away with it?

The right Sales training programs start with an explanation to the sales team of *What* and *Who*. Marketing must have prepared this information in advance, and should be present at least for the first training session. It is Marketing's responsibility to make sure this absolutely critical information is accepted, understood, and agreed upon by the trainees. Unless and until Sales gains an understanding of *What* and *Who*, your *How* training is a waste of time.

The best, real world example of this situation is a letter written to *Business Week* (October 25, 1993) by Shawn Casey, a former IBM sales professional.

"I would like to point out to Lou Gerstner that IBM's problems may be more fundamental than he thinks. As a former IBM marketing representative with 11 years' experience, every year I would ask my manager the following three questions:

Who [emphasis added] are my customers?

What [emphasis added] do you want me to sell?

How will I be paid?

My first-, second-, and third-line managers didn't have the answers."

Get your marketing professionals to figure out this hard stuff:

1. *What* can customers buy from your company they can't buy anywhere else, or that you can at least claim before others do, and

2. *Who* wants to buy it

Do that, get it right, communicate it to Sales and sales will go up, because your sales organization will at long last get better. It's just not rocket science.

[APPENDIX A]

The Marketing Process Flowchart
(see spread over page)

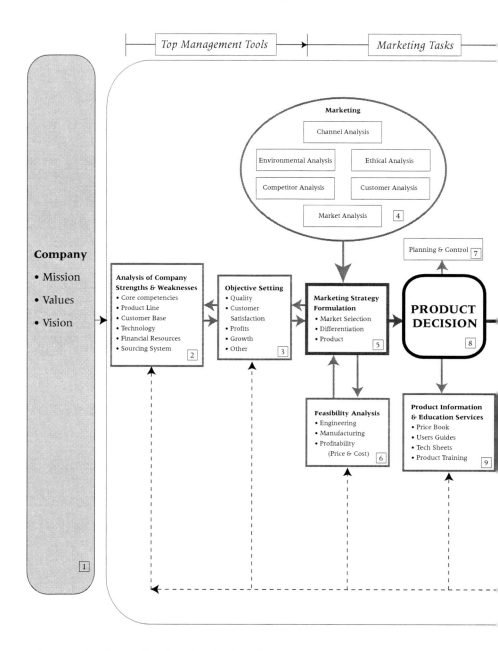

Top Management Tools → Marketing Tasks

Marketing

Channel Analysis

Environmental Analysis   Ethical Analysis

Competitor Analysis   Customer Analysis

Market Analysis   4

Company

• Mission

• Values

• Vision

1

Analysis of Company Strengths & Weaknesses
• Core competencies
• Product Line
• Customer Base
• Technology
• Financial Resources
• Sourcing System   2

Objective Setting
• Quality
• Customer Satisfaction
• Profits
• Growth
• Other   3

Marketing Strategy Formulation
• Market Selection
• Differentiation
• Product   5

Planning & Control   7

PRODUCT DECISION   8

Feasibility Analysis
• Engineering
• Manufacturing
• Profitability
  (Price & Cost)   6

Product Information & Education Services
• Price Book
• Users Guides
• Tech Sheets
• Product Training   9

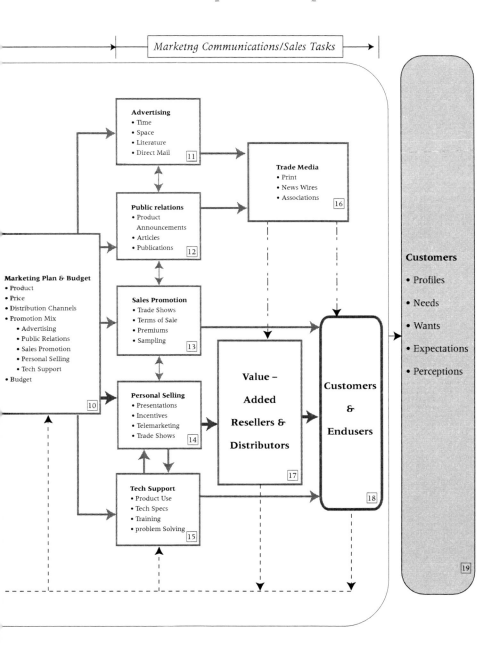

Marketng Communications/Sales Tasks

Advertising
- Time
- Space
- Literature
- Direct Mail
11

Trade Media
- Print
- News Wires
- Associations
16

Public relations
- Product Announcements
- Articles
- Publications
12

Marketing Plan & Budget
- Product
- Price
- Distribution Channels
- Promotion Mix
  - Advertising
  - Public Relations
  - Sales Promotion
  - Personal Selling
  - Tech Support
- Budget
10

Sales Promotion
- Trade Shows
- Terms of Sale
- Premiums
- Sampling
13

Value – Added Resellers & Distributors
17

Customers & Endusers
18

Customers
- Profiles
- Needs
- Wants
- Expectations
- Perceptions
19

Personal Selling
- Presentations
- Incentives
- Telemarketing
- Trade Shows
14

Tech Support
- Product Use
- Tech Specs
- Training
- problem Solving
15

[APPENDIX B]

How Can Wholesalers and Distributors Use This Secret?*

Increasing sales in a distribution company has special problems. The efficiency solutions covered in Section 1 apply to wholesalers and distributors as much as they do to manufacturers. In reality, many distributors are further down the learning curve in this efficiency area than are the manufacturers whose products they distribute.

This is amazing considering the low regard many manu-facturers have for their distributors. If most manufacturers didn't believe that distributors and wholesalers were "pond scum, who suck margin from the manufacturer," they might have opened their eyes sooner to some of these efficiency

---

* If you're reading this Appendix before you've read the book, it isn't going to make any sense. The concepts discussed in here are based on ideas presented in the body of the book.

solutions which these "lowly" distributors developed. (But enough about that or I'll be on my soap box for pages.)

Understanding *Who* and *What* for a distributor or wholesaler becomes complex because of the varying number of lines they may carry and the already noted fact in Section 2: The Secret — Revealed, that most manufacturers don't know *Who* or *What* about their own product lines. What's a distributor to do?

The Ideal Solution

One solution is to only accept lines from manufacturers who can describe their *Who* and *What* to you. This would be ideal because the manufacturer could also select distributors who really serve the known *Who*. Unfortunately, if you restrict the lines you carry to only those that are a fit for you, and whose marketing departments can describe a *Who* and a unique (or any) *What*, you'll have a very short, or non-existent, line card.

How About a Practical Idea?

Since that ideal solution doesn't seem too realistic, what else can you do? First, recognize that most manufacturers expect their distributors to create a market for the manufacturer's products. The manufacturer's expectations demand much more marketing than distributors, given their margins, can realistically provide. This isn't going to change until enough manufacturers realize what too few now know: Manufacturers can gain an unfair advantage from the channel if they don't expect the channel to do their marketing for them. (Uh oh, I'm trying to get back on the soap box.)

As a distributor, the first thing you have to try is to select products that appeal to similar *Whos*. This is fairly obvious to all distributors. Notwithstanding the obviousness of this need, too many lines end up in the hands of the wrong distributors. Why? Because, the distributor buys into the manufacturer's poorly thought out discussion of *Who* buys. Too often the manufacturer's definition of *Who* is a wish and a hope, not a fact.

An example from a few years ago is the Nenio palm computing device from Phillips. This product, using Windows CE, was designed to compete with the U.S. Robotics (or 3-Com aka Palm Computing) Palm. Given the Palm's entrenched position in the business market, it appeared that Phillips was going to try to target the home or personal user. It wasn't going to happen at $399.00. Phillips didn't have a *What* that the *Who* (consumer) would pay that price for. Given that Phillips has been on the leading edge of numerous consumer electronics products, only to have failed in their introduction (the video game and the laser disc player to name two), you'd think they'd learn to understand *What* their target *Whos* will buy at a price point. Guess not, and the channel ate it again in this case.

So, the distributor or wholesaler has to spend time questioning the manufacturer's assumptions before buying into their presumptions. This process takes some time, effort, and thinking that may not have previously been practiced extensively by the channel. It's an unfortunate necessity.

What to do about *What* is a whole different problem. Unfortunately the only solution to this problem is to badger, cajole and nag your manufacturers' marketing departments to give you a good and unique answer to this *What* question. When they finally give you what may appear to be an answer, you'll have to test it in the market. (Let's face it, it won't be the first time you've had to test market for a manufacturer. Oops, soap box slipping again.)

Give your real world feedback to the manufacturer. If they've got it right, good for them — and you. If the *What* doesn't appear to play, check with some other distributors of the manufacturer and see if they agree with your assessment. It could be your *Who* doesn't want that *What*, or it could be a bogus *What*. It pays to find out.

If This Were Easy, They Wouldn't Pay You the Big Bucks to Be a Distributor

I'd love to tell you this is a solvable problem, but it isn't completely solvable by you as a distributor. The real solution lies with the manufacturers accepting, understanding, and agreeing (to borrow from sales guru Ted Steinberg) that it's the manufacturer's primary responsibility to figure out *Who* and *What* and explain it to Sales (which includes distributors and wholesalers).

If you like what this book has to say, and you think it's a compelling message, buy a bunch of them and give them to your manufacturers' marketing, sales and senior management people. That would help both of you — and me, too.

How Can You Use *Who* and *What* to Differentiate Your Distribution Business?

Now you know some ways to use *Who* and *What* to help

you select and sell the lines you might carry. Most of that is in the hands of your suppliers. That may be helpful, but how can you use the concepts of *Who* and *What* to differentiate your actual distribution or wholesale business?

Assuming you don't have any exclusive distribution contracts, the *What* can't be your "stuff." If other distributors or wholesalers in the territory offer the same lines, then the *items* you sell can't be a differentiator. Maybe it's the breadth of your offering? That is an answer I've heard from some distributors and wholesalers.

Unfortunately, that differentiator may exist more in your mind, than in reality, but it's simple for you to determine. Take a look at the items your customers buy from you. How many of your customers actually take advantage of your "breadth of line"? If a significant percentage do, then breadth could be at least one of your differentiators. If almost all do, then you may be on to something. If virtually none of your customers do, then maybe you have a lot of different *Whos* that you're serving.

Aside from the breadth of line or selection concept, some of the other *Whats* that distributors usually mention are:

Availability

Prompt delivery

Courteous service

Price

Hours open

Knowledgeable sales people

Price

Some or all of those may be true, and there may be others that are valid in your case. To find the actual answer for your firm you must go through the same process as outlined on pages 110–113 in Section 2: The Secret — Revealed.

Final Thoughts on *Who* and *What*

Many very successful distributors and wholesalers have said (with a straight face) that there is no difference in their business. They claim they are virtually identical to other distributors in their territory. My response is always the same: So how is it that you're in business? The ensuing discussion usually results in some ideas as to what their *What* is or may be.

Of course, to find out you have to look. But one thing is sure: If you have been, or are planning to be, in business for the long term, there must be something(s) that makes you valuably different in the minds of your customers. The sooner you learn what it is, the sooner your sales force can capitalize on it. It's just not rocket science.

[ABOUT THE AUTHOR]

A recognized expert in marketing, innovation and leadership, strategic positioning, and customer relationships, Mitch Goozé has addressed groups throughout the world, winning high ratings for his energetic presentation style and results oriented approach.

His ideas have helped senior executives from more than 4,000 companies define their market niches, manage innovation, develop and implement practical, workable plans, and realign their efforts to focus more closely on the customer.

Mitch Goozé is an experienced general manager and leader with operating experience in the high technology and consumer products industries. He has experience running divisions of large companies, as well as being CEO of mid-sized companies. Mr. Goozé was president of Teledyne Components, a division of Teledyne, Inc. for five years from 1985 to 1990.

Mr. Goozé has a B.S. in Engineering from the University of California, Los Angeles. He did graduate work in electrical engineering at the California State University, Long Beach and graduate business studies at Santa Clara University. He also holds an MBA from The Edinburgh Business School, Heriot-Watt University, Edinburgh, Scotland.

Mr. Goozé is a member of the Board of Directors of Telesensory Systems. He's a past member of the Board of Directors of The American Electronics Association and ASUCLA, and The Board of Advisors of the Leavey School of Business at Santa Clara University. He is a Certified Speaking Professional (CSP) and a Founder of the International Center for Professional Speaking in Phoenix, AZ. TEC Worldwide, a Knowledge Universe company and international organization of CEOs, named him Marketing Resource of the Year.

Mitch was a major contributor to *Future In Sight*, (Macmillan, 1995) and his own book, *It's Not Rocket Science: Using Marketing to Build a Sustainable Business*, (IMI, 1997, 2002) is available in trade paperback. He has been president of Customer Manufacturing Group, Inc. since 1991. Customer Manufacturing Group helps its customers convert their marketing and sales activities into a System to Manufacture Customers®.

[INDEX]

and Sears, 105–106
Walton, Sam, 125
  and Wal-Mart, 125
Waterman, Bob, 128
Watson, Tom Jr., and IBM,
  124
Watson, Tom Sr., and IBM,
  124
Who and What. See Buying;
  Marketing-to-sales
  process; Sales
Wholesalers, 143-149
  and distributors, 143–149

and manufacturers,
  143–149
and sales
  understanding who buys,
  144-149
  understanding what the
  customer is buying,
  144-149
Wilson Learning, 18

Z
Zig Ziglar, 18